HITCHCOCK
piece by piece

HITCHCOCK
piece by piece

by
Laurent Bouzereau

foreword by
Patricia Hitchcock O'Connell

ABRAMS, New York

This book is designed and produced by
Jean-François Kowalski
KNY Studio
New York, NY

www.knystudio.com

With the further assistance of

Copy editor	*Clearance services*
Therese Eiben	Adele Sparks

Abrams coordination team

Project Manager	*Production Manager*
Aiah Rachel Wieder	Ankur Ghosh

*Cataloging-in-Publication Data has been applied for and may be obtained
from the Library of Congress.*

ISBN: 978-0-8109-9601-4

Abrams books are available at special discounts when purchased in quantity
for premiums and promotions as well as fundraising or educational use.
Special editions can also be created to specification. For details, contact
specialmarkets@abramsbooks.com or the address below.

THE ART OF BOOKS SINCE 1949

115 West 18th Street
New York, NY 10011
www.abramsbooks.com

PAGE 2 Portrait of Alfred Hitchcock from the 1920s

table *of* contents

foreword

by Patricia Hitchcock O'Connell

My father, Alfred Hitchcock, used to say when referring to his work, "It's only a movie!" Yet, when I see the continuing interest in his films, the number of books written about them, the wealth of documentaries that examine and dissect his work, not to mention the retrospectives and the showings of his work on television, I have to acknowledge that *none* of my father's films were *just* movies! In fact, even the name itself, *Alfred Hitchcock*, is no longer just a name.

How often have I heard the phrase, "It's so Hitch-cockian!" How often have *you* heard it? On television, in the course of casual conversations; we read it in newspapers, magazines, and on the Internet almost daily. It has come to mean so many things: suspense, fear, murder, ingenious camera work, creative art direction, great stories and characters, twisting plots, cameo appearances . . . the list goes on.

It's no surprise that *Hitchcockian* has multiple meanings. What falls under what my father called *movie* comprises many different elements, some having to do with pure storytelling and others with technical achievements. My father was known as the master of suspense, not only because he knew how to manipulate an audience, but also because he developed a particular language that used all the great tools the art of filmmaking had to offer. But what's remarkable is that, having started his career in the silent era in England alongside his trusted wife and colleague, Alma Reville, he invented most

of the techniques and vocabulary still in use by contemporary filmmakers.

And this is not just an admiring daughter talking, a daughter who loved both the man and the film-maker. A daughter who had the great privilege of watching him at work and who was even given the opportunity to act in some of his most memorable films (*Stage Fright*, 1950, *Strangers on a Train*, 1951, and *Psycho*, 1960). My father's creative genius has been acknowledged by everyone who ever saw one of his films, and I have yet to meet someone who didn't recognize his immense contribution to the history of cinema.

Therefore, it pleases my family and me greatly that an industry so often dismissive of its own history doesn't seem to have forgotten Alfred Hitchcock. In film, achieving artistic success is a rare feat. Doing so while maintaining popularity presents an altogether different challenge. Being immortalized through one's artistic creations is something most of us can only dream of. In the case of my father, I can honestly say that, without even really trying, he has entered the pantheon of unforgettable artists.

However, the thing that I think would surprise my father and my mother the most would not be getting the Oscar he never received in his lifetime, or reading about the profound effect his work had on successive generations of filmmakers, or realizing that critics and film historians who may have initially dismissed him because his films were commercial have been

PAGE 9 With the family's Sealyham terrier at Patricia's wedding, 1952

proven wrong about the everlasting power of his work. What would please Alfred Hitchcock and Alma Reville the most is the fact that year after year, decade after decade, his films continue to seduce audiences. The public's reaction really was first and foremost what he cared about. Knowing that *Psycho* is still as terrifying as it was when it first came out; that *Rear Window* (1954) has not aged one bit; that *North by Northwest* (1959) is still a thrill ride; that *The Birds* (1963) is perhaps more accepted today than it was when it first appeared on the screen—these testaments to the durability of his artistic vision would please him and my mother to no end. Very few filmmakers, very few artists have had that privilege, and I am thrilled that his films live on and remain fresh in everyone's mind. I am also convinced that the connection he had with the audience through his films is something that will never die.

When the idea of participating in yet another book highlighting my father's films arose, I felt it had to have a fresh new approach. In an age where most everything exists in the virtual world, the concept of an interactive, hands-on journey through the creative genesis of my father's films seemed inspired. This book reproduces actual mementos that are separate from the text. Readers can pull letters out of envelopes, handle photographs and sketches, and unfold personal documents that were part of my father's thought process and work method. This approach represents the ultimate and definitive tribute to the Hitchcock legacy, because, dear reader and audience member, it enables you to relive my father's creative process through faithful reproductions of elements that led to the making of his films. So it is my great pleasure to welcome you to what I consider to be a Hitchcock museum, one that will help keep the Hitchcock legacy alive and will make you want to rediscover the films with deeper insight into their making. My father would have been thrilled with this creative presentation of his work. In fact, I think he would have said, "I thought I directed *just* movies. But this is *not just* a book!"

— Patricia Hitchcock O'Connell

LEFT With Patricia and Joseph E. O'Connell, Jr., bride and groom, 1952

ABOVE With Patricia Hitchcock and Mary, her first of three daughters, 1953

birth of a filmmaker

INTRODUCTION

*Shortly after the idea of filmmaking
was conceived, along came Alfred Hitchcock*

RIGHT AND PAGES 14–17 Alma Reville and Hitchcock in Bavaria during the filming
of *The Pleasure Garden* (1925), the first movie directed by Hitchcock

How fitting that Alfred Joseph Hitchcock's birth, on August 13, 1899, nearly coincides with the conception of the motion picture era. Hitch— as his friends and colleagues would later call him— was the third child of William Hitchcock, a grocer, and Emma Jane Whelan. The Catholic family (young Alfred Hitchcock went to a Jesuit school) lived in Leytonstone, an area in East London. The grocery store and family home where Hitch lived with his parents, his older brother, William (born 1890), and sister, Eileen (born 1892), was located at 517 High Road, but the father regularly traveled to Covent Garden to buy his fruits and vegetables at the great marketplace there. For any Hitchcock fan, Covent Garden immediately evokes the setting of *Frenzy* (1972), Hitchcock's penultimate film. To make it, Hitch returned to England and despite the circumstances of the story (women being raped and strangled, with one of the victims being shoved in a potato bag), the film really was a nostalgic look at the area where Alfred Hitchcock strolled around as a boy.

As this book offers a thematic approach to Hitchcock's work, it's interesting to point out as we evoke his boyhood that even though there is nothing childish about a Hitchcock film, children were present in several of his best titles. Kids in Hitch's films are often mischievous, clever, and truth-tellers. One of Hitchcock's most notable early cameo appearances (in his first sound picture, *Blackmail*, 1929) takes place on the subway, where a boy is pestering him. Many years later, for his cameo appearance in *Torn Curtain*, one of his last films, the director has a (wet!) baby on his lap. But children had more consequential roles, too, as in the first version of *The Man Who Knew Too Much* (1934). In the film, Nova Pilbeam plays Betty, the young girl who is kidnapped. Two decades later in the remake (1956), her boy equivalent, Christopher Olsen as Hank, not only got more screen time, including dancing and singing with his mom, played by the ever charming Doris Day, he also instigates the plot: on a bus trip to Marrakech with his parents (James Stewart plays the dad), he accidentally pulls a veil from a woman's face. An argument with the woman's husband ensues until the family is rescued by a French traveler played by Daniel Gélin, a mysterious man who is in fact an agent (and later shows up with a knife in his back). The boy's funniest remark in the film is one that you could have heard from Hitchcock's own lips: when referring to the snails in his parents' garden, the boy says, "We tried everything to get rid of them. We never thought of a Frenchman!"

In *Young and Innocent* (1938), the constable's daughter, played by an older Nova Pilbeam, looks after her kid brothers while falling in love with a man falsely accused of murder. In that film, there's a fun sequence that takes place at a children's birthday party. Years later Hitchcock would decide to showcase a dramatic attack on children at an outdoor birthday party in *The Birds*. There are also the kids from Hitchcock's own favorite film, *Shadow of a Doubt* (1943). Teresa Wright plays Charlie, a teenager infatuated with and admiring of her Uncle Charlie, after whom she is named. (Uncle Charlie is brilliantly played by Joseph Cotten.) Young Charlie comes of age quickly and abruptly when she discovers that her uncle is in fact "The Merry Widow Murderer." She has a little brother ("the spoilt one!" as he is lovingly nicknamed by his mother, played by the delicious Patricia Collinge) and a younger sister, Ann, whose goal in life is "to correct her elders." Ann is played by Edna May

Wonacott, who rehearsed lines and prepared for the part during production with the master's daughter herself, Patricia Hitchcock. There's no wonder the little girl in *Shadow of a Doubt* has a twinkle in her eye. Ann is an avid reader and, armed with the knowledge she gleans from all the good and historical literature she reads, she has ample opportunity to show off her precocity, unlike her father, played by Henry Travers, who prefers the world of detective novels. Perhaps that's why she alone seems to intuit that Uncle Charlie is not who he pretends to be.

In *Saboteur* (1942), Hitchcock directs a baby girl to playfully toss just-delivered mail to Barry Kane (Robert Cummings), a man wrongly accused of sabotage. The return address on one of the letters incriminates the baby's grandfather as a traitor. In *Strangers on a Train* (1951), we see how cruel Bruno Anthony (Robert Walker) is when he pops a little boy's balloon with his cigarette. And later as Bruno fights with Guy Haines (Farley Granger) on a merry-go-round gone wild, a boy next to them is laughing, unaware that a life-and-death duel is going on. In *Stage Fright* (1950), a boy scout armed with a bloodied doll is employed to get Charlotte Inwood (Marlene Dietrich) to implicate herself in the murder of her husband. In *I Confess* (1953), Hitchcock leaves it to two young girls to say they saw a priest escape from the scene of a crime, which increases the chances of Father Logan (Montgomery Clift) being accused (wrongly) of murder. And again in *The Birds*, Melanie Daniels (Tippi Hedren) uses the excuse of bringing love birds as a birthday gift to the kid sister of Mitch Brenner (Rod Taylor) in order to connect with him romantically.

And so on . . .

But one (personal) favorite is Arnie as played by *Leave It To Beaver* star Jerry Mathers in the dark comedy about a corpse, *The Trouble With Harry* (1955). Arnie is irresistibly funny, but, "don't try to make sense out of him," his mother (played by Shirley MacLaine in her first screen role) says, "he's got his own timing!" He'll trade you a dead rabbit for blueberry muffins, but above all, he is the one who first stumbles across Harry—and Harry is dead. Curiously, the kid isn't really shocked by the sight of the dead man. Perhaps he knows "it's only a movie!" Alfred Hitchcock may not have been like Arnie growing up, but, as he proved not only in his films and in the now-classic introductions to his television shows, he most certainly shared with him a dead-pan humor.

But beyond those fictional kids, getting back to the director's own childhood, there's the infamous story of young Alfred Hitchcock who, having done something wrong, was taken by his father to the local jail and put behind bars for a few minutes while being told, "This is what we do to naughty boys." Hence the director's admitted lifelong fear of policemen—and possibly the provenance of his fascination with the macabre that led him to explore what real naughty boys were like. On a more profound and personal level, this single event may have triggered Hitch's cinematic investigation of the wrong man, the anti-hero who is found at the center of so many Hitchcock classics.

The wrong man is just one thematic connection among the films of Alfred Hitchcock. Not surprisingly, when considering the brilliant mind that set his films in motion, there are several recurrent subjects that seem to have preoccupied the man. And that is the proposed journey for this book. Along with the selected documents and photos, it was essential to find a different way to approach the Hitchcock oeuvre. A chronology seemed banal, but what if the great master of suspense himself were still alive and the opportunity to interview him about his entire body of work were possible? How would the discussion begin? A few words about his childhood, his marriage to the talented Alma Reville, not only his lifelong companion, but also a colleague and his most trusted partner-in-film.

But then the discussion would very quickly focus on the films and the many themes that fascinated the great Hitchcock brain, including his now-archetypal leading character, the wrong man; the complexities women—blondes, brunettes, and mothers—bring to his films; the psychos and other villains who are brought so vividly to life; and of course the myriad signature filmic innovations and images that resonate today as *Hitchcockian*. (By choice, we will explore the film world of Alfred Hitchcock, not his television series.)

Alfred Hitchcock once said, "I want to be remembered as a man who entertained millions through the technique of film." As this book will confirm, he not only succeeded in entertaining millions, but also he educated, taught, and continues to captivate everyone who has ever wondered, "What is a movie?" What follows is one possible answer.

wrong men and anti-heroes

CHAPTER I

Hitchcock's archetypal leading man,
wrong place, wrong time

"My hero is always the average man to whom bizarre things happen, rather than vice versa," Alfred Hitchcock once declared. In summing up his leading men, he said his goal was to take the ordinary man, throw him in an extraordinary situation, "and keep him there." Is there a more suspense-laden situation for an average man to find himself in than to be falsely accused of a crime? Of *murder*? Perhaps, but judging by the number of times Hitchcock employed that particular plot twist, the director seems to have thought it resonated with his audiences' deepest fears—and perhaps even his own. Over his many years of filmmaking, Hitchcock returned time again to the "wrong man" set-up, beginning with the first real Hitchcock thriller, *The Lodger: A Story of the London Fog* (1927).

Where was Hitchcock in his life and career at the time of this project? He had gone to the School of Engineering and Navigation in London, where he trained as a draughtsman. This led to a job as a technical clerk at the W. T. Henley Telegraph Company. For medical reasons, Hitch received a C3 Classification, which kept him from military service during World War I, but he joined the volunteer corps of the Royal Engineers. Throughout all of this change and upheaval, Hitchcock said he remained "deeply interested in film," a passion that began "from about twelve or fourteen on." In 1919, when Famous Players-Lasky, an American film company that would eventually become Paramount, decided to establish an operation in Islington, a borough of London, Hitch saw an opportunity that could fulfill his interest. Hitchcock approached the company, was convincing enough to be invited to join the crew, and officially began his career in film by designing title cards. (Remember, it was still the silent-film era.) He expressed his interest in directing and nearly got his chance with a film called *Number 13*. Unfortunately, the title would indeed mean plain bad luck for Hitch, as the project remained unfinished. An uncertain period followed when Famous Players-Lasky abandoned its British operation. Hitchcock connected with Seymour Hicks, an actor-producer who, having noticed the young man's enthusiasm, hired him to complete a film after the original director dropped out. Hitch's contribution to the film *Always Tell the Wife* (1923) went uncredited.

When the studios at Islington were taken over by Balcon/Freeman/Saville, Hitchcock worked there again in various capacities, gaining experience as screenwriter, art director, and assistant director. Most significantly, it was there that he met his future wife, Alma Reville, who, it should be said, at that point had more experience and was higher up the cinematic ladder than Hitch.

They worked together on several films, most of them directed by Graham Cutts, who noticed Hitchcock's skills and quickly became threatened by his talent. Despite that challenge, Hitchcock finally got his first chance at directing with *The Pleasure Garden* (1925), followed by *The Mountain Eagle* (1927), thanks to producer Michael Balcon, for Gainsborough Films (a company Balcon had formed with Graham Cutts). Cutts hated the films and, having the power to do so, had them shelved. Neither film would be released until the success of Hitchcock's first thriller, *The Lodger* (1927).

The story, based on the 1913 novel by Marie Belloc Lowndes, takes place in London, where a serial killer known as the "Avenger," who attacks only blondes, is on the loose. One night, a man arrives to stay in a family-run boarding house. The owners' daughter, a blonde, likes the lodger, but her parents are troubled by his behavior: He seems to go out only at night, and he has removed the portraits of young women from the bedroom walls. Believing him to be the Avenger, the couple has the lodger arrested. He escapes wearing handcuffs and is chased and nearly lynched by a mad crowd. When the real killer is apprehended,

LEFT Cameraman Jack Cox and Hitchcock (far right) on the set of *The Ring* (1927)

ABOVE Ivor Novello and the actress known as June in *The Lodger* (1927)

the lodger's innocence is revealed. In fact, he was looking to avenge the murder of his own sister. The film ends with the lodger in the arms of the woman whose family nearly got him killed!

The interesting aspect of this early exploration of Hitchcock's leading theme is that we, the audience, are put in the same position as the characters in the film. We're not sure that the lodger is innocent. He may be the killer. That alone, of course, enhances the suspense, and Hitchcock, in that early film, already displays his gift for audience manipulation. In the novel, which borrows from the Jack the Ripper case, the lodger *is* the killer. This was, of course, an unacceptable ending, particularly if one considers that the then-wildly popular movie star Ivor Novello played the lead.

The Lodger was silent and showed how much Hitchcock had learned during his time in Germany, where the earlier films he worked on were made. The director often cited the influence German cinema had on his visual style. The film included innovative camera angles, lighting, and imaginative visual tricks. For one of the most memorable scenes, Hitchcock had a ceiling built out of glass. When the owners of the boarding house look up to the ceiling that connects to the room where the mysterious lodger is staying, we get to "see through" his privacy and observe the man nervously pacing.

ABOVE Hitchcock doing his cameo appearance in *Blackmail*, his first talkie (1929)
RIGHT Hitchcock, with hands on hips, on the set of *Rich and Strange* (1932)

Although *The Lodger* was eventually lauded as "the finest British production ever made," the road to success was detoured by professional jealousy. The film was bad-mouthed by Graham Cutts and shelved for a time. On release, it was enthusiastically received.

Hitchcock didn't return to the theme of the wrong man (although *Murder!* in 1930 did have a wrong *woman*) for another eight years when he turned his attention to *The 39 Steps* (1935), starring the unforgettable Robert Donat. During the intervening time he made two more films for Gainsborough with Michael Balcon as producer, *Downhill* (1927) and *Easy Virtue* (1927). He left Gainsborough that year and went to British International Pictures, where most of his films were produced by John Maxwell. At BIP Hitchcock directed *The Ring* (1927), *The Farmer's Wife* (1928), *Champagne* (1928), *The*

Manxman (1929), *Blackmail* (Hitch's and Britain's first sound picture, 1929), *Elstree Calling* (1930), *Juno and the Paycock* (1930), *Murder!* (1930), *The Skin Game* (1931), *Number Seventeen* (1932), and *Rich and Strange* (1932). In 1933, Hitch made his only musical, *Waltzes from Vienna*.

By this time Michael Balcon, Hitchcock's producer on *The Lodger*, had become director of production at Gaumont-British. He offered Hitchcock a contract, which Hitch accepted, initiating a historically creative period in the director's oeuvre. Beginning with *The Man Who Knew Too Much* (1934), Hitchcock went on to make his best films yet for Gaumont-British (three of them produced by Balcon). These films established the themes that Hitchcock later explored in his American films, after producer David O. Selznick brought him to America.

For those who had missed *The Lodger, The 39 Steps* is probably one of the most defining early Hitchcock films. Robert Donat played Richard Hannay, a Canadian tourist who meets a young woman at a London music hall. She comes home with him after convincing him that she is in danger—and winds up dying with a knife in her back, but not before telling him about a plot involving a spy ring known as the 39 Steps. Subsequently, Hannay is accused of her murder and is forced to stop the plot if he wants to clear his name.

"I know what it is to feel lonely and helpless and to have the whole world against me, and those are things no men or women ought to feel," Hannay declares at one point to a crowd that thinks he is a city official delivering a speech. It is an eloquent defense of the *wrong man*! Years later, Hannay's plight influenced characters played by Cary Grant in *North by Northwest* (1959) and *To Catch a Thief* (1955). Roger O. Thornhill in *North by Northwest* is

mistaken for an agent and accused (like Hannay) of stabbing someone. In Thornhill's case the stakes are even higher; his supposed victim is a delegate to the United Nations. In *To Catch a Thief*, Cary Grant portrays John Robie, a "retired" jewel thief who is framed by the real thief. At one point Robie says to Grace Kelly's character, who doesn't believe in his innocence, "You don't have to spend every day of your life proving your honesty, but I do."

Beyond the concept of being "wronged," Hitch's heroes share something else. Something that was very much part of Hitchcock's own personality and became one of his trademarks: a sense of humor. Obviously, Hannay in *The 39 Steps* and Thornhill and Robie, respectively, in *North by Northwest* and *To Catch a Thief* are disturbed by the injustice they suffer, yet all three characters maintain good humor throughout their plights. This makes them highly likeable. A classic line comes from Grant in *North by Northwest* when he thinks he has caught on to Kaplan, the man the villains are really after (and who, as it turns out, doesn't even exist). He breaks into "Kaplan's" room at the Plaza Hotel and, looking through his wardrobe, he nonchalantly concludes, "They must have mistaken me for a much shorter man!"

Unlike *North by Northwest*, which was an original screenplay by Ernest Lehman, *The 39 Steps* was Charles Bennett's adaptation of the 1915 John Buchan novel. In the film, Hannay is very much the bachelor that Cary Grant would portray later in *North by Northwest* (Thornhill has been divorced twice) and in *To Catch a Thief*. All three characters share a playful, carefree quality, but as their journeys to prove their innocence twist and turn, they mature and become

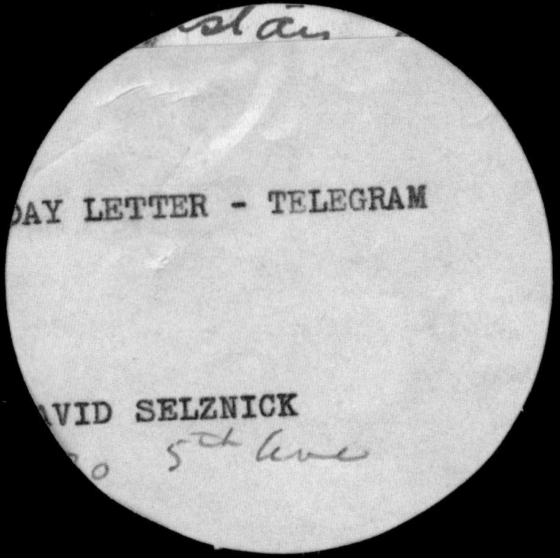

HITCHCOCK
piece by piece

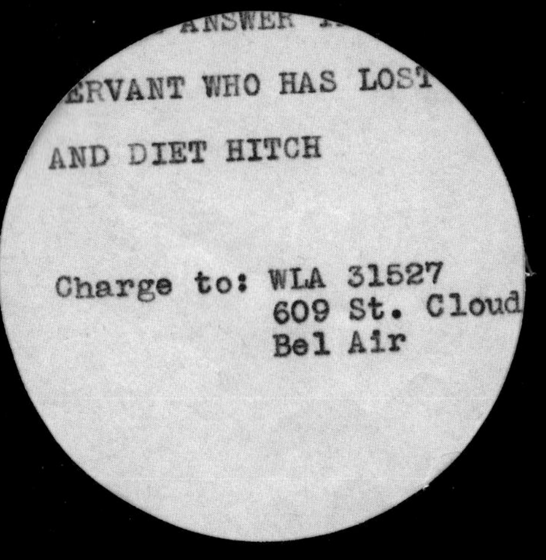

DAY LETTER - TELEGRAM

AVID SELZNICK
5th Ave

ANSWER
ERVANT WHO HAS LOST
AND DIET HITCH

Charge to: WLA 31527
609 St. Cloud
Bel Air

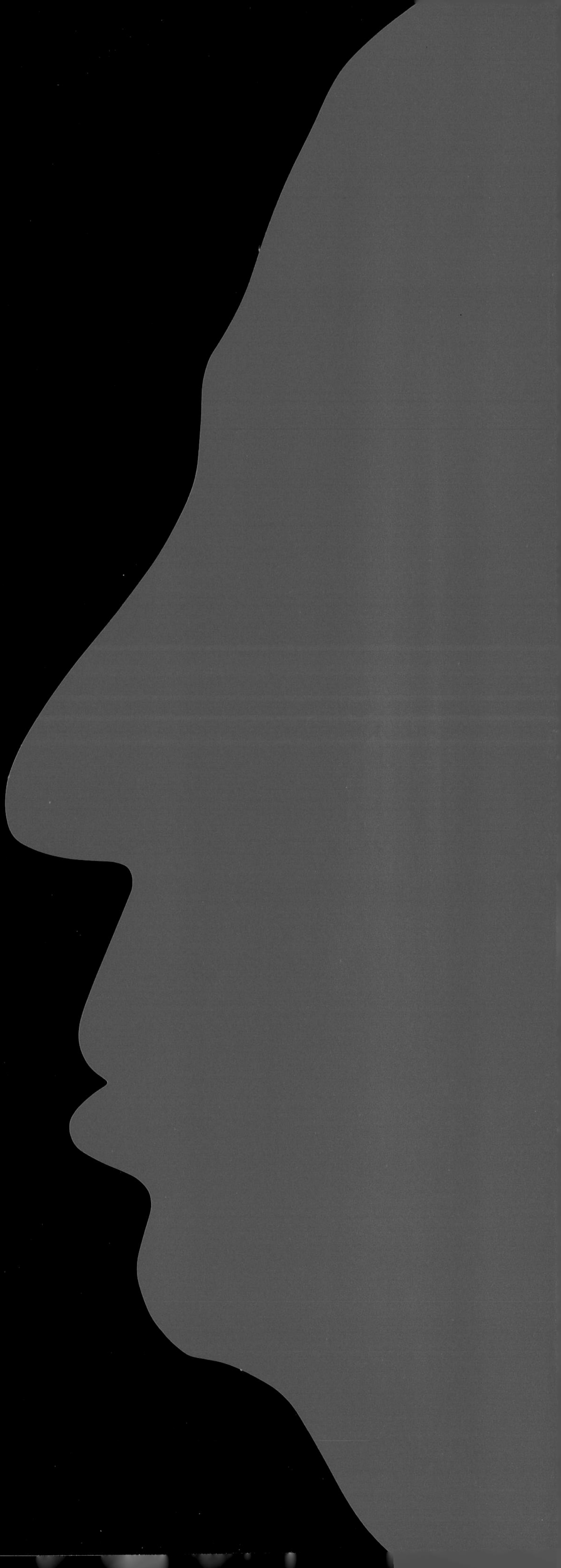

HITCHCOCK
piece by piece

more responsible. A false accusation starts each of them on the road to self-discovery, triggered by what Hitchcock called the *MacGuffin*.

The *MacGuffin* refers to an often-unspecified notion of what the bad guys are after. The MacGuffin drives the action, but never gets clearly defined because we, as the audience, don't really care—and we're not supposed to. We care only that justice is done and that the wrong man be declared innocent. Particularly in *The 39 Steps* and *North by Northwest*, the plot and what the spies are after become irrelevant to the wrong man's quest for justice.

Clearly, Hitchcock had great affection for his wrong men. He put them into awful situations, but they had a lot to learn on the way to proving their innocence. Another classic example is *Young and*

Innocent (1938). In that film a young man (Derrick de Marney), who is accused of strangling an actress, falls in love with the constable's daughter (Nova Pilbeam). Together, with the help of a homeless man (Percy Marmont), they manage to find the real killer (George Curzon), a band musician with twitching eyes. Our wrong man here follows the same path as Donat in *The 39 Steps*. He never seems quite affected by the circumstances of his situation and embraces the journey with an almost perverse sense of joy. When the constable's daughter says to him, "Don't you know what it means if you're caught?" he replies with a joke: "I'll make a rough guess…horribly rough!" She doesn't think it's funny, but he does. "I can laugh because I'm innocent," he says. More important to Robert Tisdall, de Marney's character, than proving

his innocence to the world is proving his innocence to the girl he has fallen in love with—and having her believe him. As with Donat's character in *The 39 Steps* and Grant's in *To Catch a Thief*, the girl is the ultimate reward, not some treasure, secret, object, or MacGuffin.

Saboteur (1942) was perceived by many, including Hitchcock himself, as an American remake of *The 39 Steps*. In it, an aircraft factory worker named Barry Kane is accused of sabotage and of starting a fire that caused the death of his best friend. Kane, played by Robert Cummings, has a good idea who the guilty man is, and he sets out on a journey to clear his name. In the course of doing so, he uncovers a plot of frightening proportions. After the project was turned down by several studios, Hitchcock ended up on loan, "courtesy of David O. Selznick," to Universal, which would, many years later, become Hitchcock's home base.

Barry Kane is one of Hitchcock's most sympathetic wrong men. Unlike Thornhill in *North by Northwest*, Robie in *To Catch a Thief*, or even Hannay in *The 39 Steps*, Kane is a serious man. For the lead, Hitchcock wanted Gary Cooper, who had already turned him down for the lead in *Foreign Correspondent* (1940). Again, he couldn't get him. Robert Cummings eventually got the part—and is quite convincing in the role. Cummings would later play the part of Grace Kelly's lover in *Dial M for Murder* (1954).

The seriousness of *Saboteur* is understandable, especially when one considers that, when the film was released, America was at war. Hitchcock admitted that he was not completely satisfied with the film. Perhaps there were too many ideas. He

LEFT Robert Cummings and Priscilla Lane in *Saboteur* (1942)

ABOVE On the set during the filming of *Saboteur*

confessed that he wasn't disciplined enough during production. But one can disagree with the master's own evaluation of his work. *Saboteur* is, on many levels, an excellent film. The story stands out because of its treatment of the wrong man. On his journey, Kane meets people from different backgrounds. The first is a truck driver who deceives the police so he can escape. Next he meets a blind man who can sense that Barry is in trouble and instinctively knows he is innocent. Eventually, Barry is forced to hide aboard a circus convoy and is put on trial, not by a court of law, but by a group of playacting performers who find him not guilty. It is clearly the working class that stands on the side of the underdog. But the ultimate verdict on Barry's innocence is delivered by the traitor himself, the one who caused him to be accused of a crime he didn't commit: "He is noble, fine, and pure. And the pure must pay in this world. He is misjudged by everyone. Even the police have a completely erroneous impression of him." In *Saboteur*, one could easily say that Barry Kane stands for the innocent victims of war and government treachery. Barry's journey is not merely personal, but resonates universally, and—dare we say—it still does.

Despite the effective Everyman quality conveyed through Kane's character, "Bob Cummings has suffered from the comparison to the other Hitchcock leading men, and I always thought it was unfair," said Norman Lloyd, who played the villain in *Saboteur*. Cummings was indeed wonderful in the part. He played it with "a very light sense about him," an effective and at times comedic simplicity and honesty that was essential for his role. Plus, Cummings's down-to-earth hero was perfect for a movie released the year America entered World War II.

Cary Grant's first role for Hitchcock was Johnny Aysgarth in *Suspicion* (1941). As the title suggests, it is yet another case of Hitch's wrong man. But this character belongs in that category by pure luck. Hitchcock originally wanted the character to actually be a killer, rather than merely a suspect, but studio heads believed audiences wouldn't accept it, and so Johnny Aysgarth got a reprieve and became a wrong man. *Suspicion* is the story of a mousy spinster named Lina McLaidlaw (Joan Fontaine) who falls in love with the irresistible Aysgarth, a seemingly rich playboy. Although they're complete opposites, they seem to connect on an emotional level and eventually marry. Soon, Lina comes to understand that Johnny is just a child at heart—a penniless child. He lies to her and continues to gamble, falling deeper in debt. His best friend is a rich but sickly man named Beaky (Nigel Bruce). Johnny immediately comes under suspicion when Beaky dies just as Johnny was due to repay the money he owed him. Everyone suspects Johnny, even Lina. And when Johnny brings her a glass of milk one night, Lina is convinced he is poisoning her in order to collect life insurance. Is Johnny guilty or is Johnny the wrong man?

Hitchcock's idea was that at the end of the film, Johnny would indeed bring a glass of milk laced with poison to Lina. But before drinking it, Lina would give him a letter addressed to her mother to mail. In the letter Lina reveals that her husband has murdered her. The film would have ended with Johnny mailing the letter, unaware of its content and of his now compromised future.

The story was based on a novel entitled *Before the Fact* by Francis Iles (the pseudonym of Anthony Berkeley, a writer of detective stories), published in

RIGHT With Cary Grant on the set of *Suspicion* (1941)

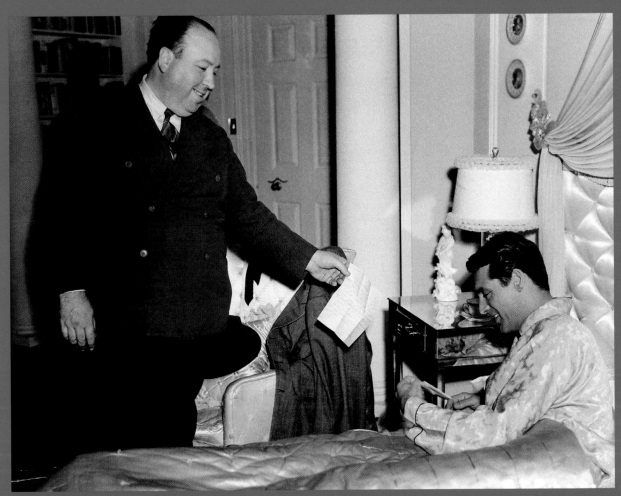
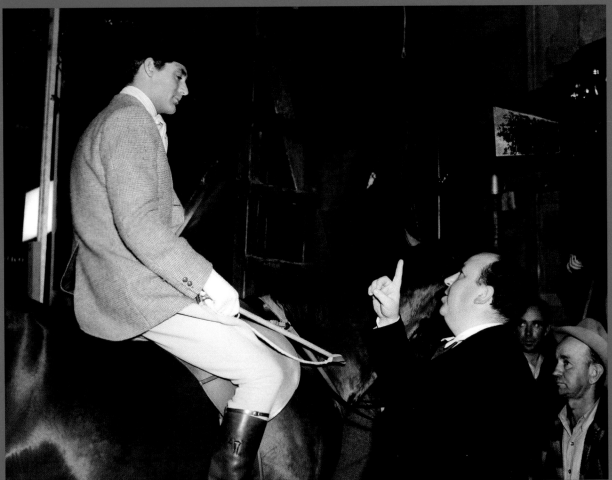

1932. The intriguing title implies that the wife, who lets her husband kill her even though she knows she is about to be his next victim, is the accessory to her own murder. In a sense, by letting him kill her, she is committing suicide. In the book, the killer goes unpunished. The problem with the novel, which was owned by RKO, was that it dealt with two subjects forbidden under the rules of the Production Code of the time: a criminal going unpunished and suicide.

When Hitchcock got involved with the project, several scripts had already been written. None were satisfactory. Hitchcock got going on a new screenplay with his wife, Alma Reville, and his assistant and collaborator, Joan Harrison. Later Samson Raphaelson, who wrote the play *The Jazz Singer*, was brought in and filming got underway. But it proved to be difficult to find a good ending for the film. Although it was set-

tled that Aysgarth would be innocent of any crime (other than being a liar and a gambler with bad luck), test audiences didn't care for a conclusion in which Lina seemed unforgivably weak for staying with a man she suspected might want to kill her. At one point, Sol Lesser, the head of RKO asked for the removal of all hints that Aysgarth could be even *suspected* of being a killer, a futile exercise which resulted in an unreleasable shorter version. Eventually, Hitchcock found the ending in the editing room—with Lina realizing that her husband was only guilty of being a frivolous spender.

Maxim de Winter (also known as Max), the character played by Laurence Olivier in *Rebecca* (1940), the first American film by Hitchcock, would also have ended up a killer, had the script followed the book.

ABOVE AND RIGHT With Gregory Peck and Ingrid Bergman on the set of *Spellbound* (1945)

In the novel by Daphne du Maurier, Max de Winter reveals that he killed his wife. Since this was not acceptable, Hitchcock turned Max into a man wrongly suspected of killing his wife. Her death was explained by Max that she tripped during a quarrel and died. The second Mrs. de Winter (played by Joan Fontaine) comes to the realization that her husband is innocent: "... but you didn't kill her, it was an accident." To which he replies, "Who would believe me?" Indeed, that's the dilemma the Hitchcock wrong man consistently faces.

The psychology of the wrong man runs deep in Hitchcock's *Spellbound* (1945). The film is based on a novel called *The House of Doctor Edwardes* by Francis Beeding (pseudonym of co-authors John

Leslie Palmer and Hilary Aidan St. George Sanders), published in England in 1927 and a year later in the United States. It was the story of a madman who locks up the director of an asylum and assumes his position. He is eventually unmasked by Dr. Constance Sedgwick. Hitchcock was interested in psychotherapy (he explored it in several of his films, most notably *Psycho*, 1960, and *Marnie*, 1964), as was his producer David O. Selznick, who hired his own shrink-to-the-stars, May Romm, M.D., as a consultant on the film. Angus MacPhail worked on the adaptation, and then Ben Hecht stepped in for research. Hitch and Hecht toured mental institutions in Connecticut, Westchester County, New York, and New York City's own Bellevue Hospital. The research and script revision resulted in a love story between

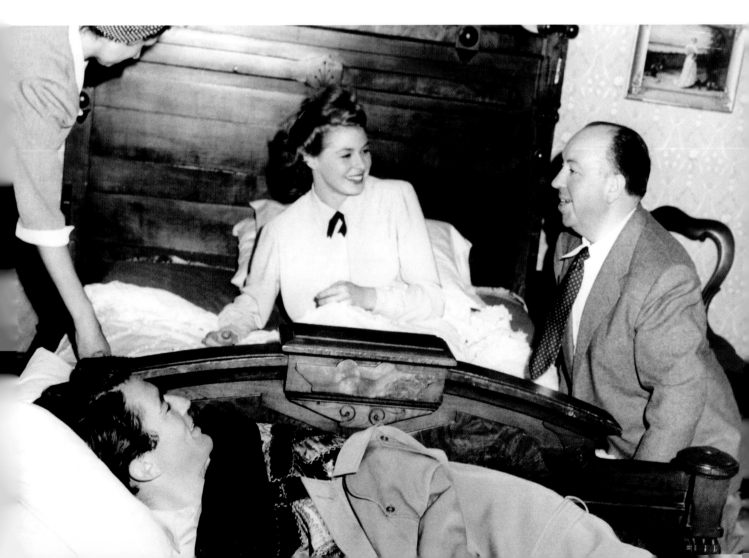

Dr. Constance Peterson (Ingrid Bergman) and John Ballantyne (Gregory Peck), an amnesiac who eventually remembers causing his brother's accidental death. Ballantyne, while still an amnesiac, poses as Doctor Edwardes, who in fact has been shot dead by his rival, Dr. Murchison. When Ballantyne is revealed to be an impostor, he is accused of killing Edwardes and becomes the wrong man. Through psychoanalysis, Constance helps Ballantyne realize that he is innocent. Ballantyne is different from other Hitchcock wrong men because, as he declares, "I'm someone else, I don't know who!" Part of the suspense is the discovery of Ballantyne's past, a past that reveals whether he is the wrong man or not. What sets him apart is that he believes he is guilty! Hitchcock later cast Gregory Peck in *The Paradine Case* (1947). In that film he hardly played a wrong man—he is the attorney to a defendant, Mrs. Paradine, accused of poisoning her husband. But in both cases, Peck plays a weak, troubled man. In *The Paradine Case*, he falls in love with his client and refuses to accept her guilt. His wife, played by Ann Todd, sees what has happened, and like Ingrid Bergman in *Spellbound*, is there to rescue him when he falls.

Patricia Highsmith, the acclaimed author of the Ripley series and other novels of suspense, wrote *Strangers on a Train,* published in 1951. Its premise was fiendishly simple. Two men meet on a train and decide to swap murders. One, Guy Haines, is not serious; he thinks it's a joke. The other, Bruno Anthony, takes the bargain seriously, carrying out his side of the deal by murdering Guy's wife. Bruno then expects Guy to kill his father as they had discussed. Guy refuses and is wrongly accused of murdering his

wife; he can't go to the police for fear that Bruno will say they planned the murder together.

Although the movie departs from the novel, the central idea remains. One can see why Hitchcock loved the storyline. It ties in with his wrong man fascination, *and* it flirts with the idea of split personality. True, Guy Haines is innocent. He didn't kill his wife, who refused to divorce him. But if one sees Bruno as Guy's dark side, his alter ego, Guy is in fact guilty. Hitchcock has a great time setting this up, staging a scene with Guy screaming over the phone to his new girlfriend that he could strangle his wife.

Hitchcock bought the rights to the novel (having become producer as well as director, he was fully in control of the material he owned) and wrote a treatment with Whitfield Cook. They changed several elements of the novel. Guy Haines becomes a tennis champion instead of an architect, and, most importantly, Guy doesn't kill Bruno's father as he does in the book—although in the film, when Guy visits Bruno's home, you think for a moment that he may have decided to do it. Instead, Guy is, as all of Hitchcock's wrong men, proven innocent. There is a bit of a moral ambiguity in this film, however: Guy wanted to get rid of his wife and, in a sense, he got what he wanted.

Farley Granger, who plays Guy in his second role with Hitchcock (his first was in *Rope* in 1948), found out about the film when Hitchcock called and asked him to visit him at his home on Bellagio Road in Beverly Hills. Hitch told him the story of *Strangers on a Train* and then asked if he liked the story. Granger said he thought it was terrific, and Hitchcock replied, "Good, we start filming on Monday in Washington, D.C.!" Not much prep was necessary for Granger. No

RIGHT Hitchcock doing his cameo appearance with Farley Granger in *Strangers on a Train* (1951)

time really. He was believable as a tennis player, since he played frequently on a court at Charlie Chaplin's house. Once they were on set, Granger said, "I remember seeing him in his chair beside the set on the second day of shooting, and he looked very down. And I said, 'Hitch, what's the matter?' and he said, 'Oh, I'm so bored . . . I've done it all. Now all I have to do is tell you where to go and tell the camera what to do." In other words, and as Cary Grant observed, "He had his picture all finished before we even arrived."

Hitchcock had only this to say about his Jesuit education: "I was scared to hell the whole time I was there. Maybe that's how I learned fear." And with *I Confess* (1953), Hitchcock got a chance to set—and test—his wrong man theory against a religious

backdrop. Otto Keller (O. E. Hasse), the caretaker of a church, confesses to a priest, Father Michael Logan (Montgomery Clift), that he murdered a man named Villette while trying to steal from him. Forbidden by the Church to reveal anything heard in the confessional, Logan cannot tell the police who the murderer is. The police, in turn, accuse Father Logan of the murder when they learn that Villette, a lawyer, was blackmailing a prominent politician's wife, Ruth Grandfort (Anne Baxter), because of a relationship she had had with Logan before he became a priest.

Logan is, simply by being a priest, one of Hitchcock's most passive wrong men. The director's interest in the story may have been the opportunity to skewer some of the more intransigent customs of the Church. The film was based on a play called *Nos Deux*

Consciences by Paul Anthelme (pseudonym of Paul Bourde) that Hitchcock had seen in the thirties. The play had a darker ending, concluding with the priest going to the guillotine for a crime he didn't commit. When Hitchcock started working on the adaptation, he knew he had to connect the priest to the victim, so he turned Villette into a blackmailer who knew of Logan's relationship with Ruth. Hitchcock also felt there should be an illegitimate child—all of this happening before Logan became a priest. When the Production Code at the time reviewed the drafts of the script, however, it raised issues with Hitchcock's approach. So Hitchcock had to give up the illegitimate child and the idea that the priest should die at the end. Instead, Logan goes on trial and is judged not guilty for lack of evidence. On his way out of the court-house, a crowd assembles against him. At that point

the killer's wife, who knows her husband murdered Villette, reveals the truth. Logan is finally free, never having had to break the rules of confession.

Despite the fact that Montgomery Clift and Hitchcock didn't particularly get along, he was the perfect choice for the part of Father Logan. He brought credibility to the situation. Played by some-one else it may have come off as contrived or even ridiculous. Clift expressed guilt, torment, and inner turmoil. He was himself a complicated man. He researched the part intensely, was in analysis at the time, and had long been concerned with spiritual matters. Clift was a "Method" actor, a technique in which actors immerse themselves into the characters they portray. And although his technique was effective on the screen, Clift may have looked for more direction and personal support from Hitchcock than the director was willing to indulge. For instance, when Hitch asked Clift to look up as he exits the courtroom after the trial or to walk across a room at the end of the film when the real killer is about to get caught, the actor wanted to know what his motivation was. "When an actor comes to me and wants to discuss his character," Hitchcock once said, "I say, 'It's in the script.' If he says, 'But what's my motivation?' I say, 'Your salary!'" Hitchcock thought cinematically. He knew how the film was going to be edited and put together. He didn't necessarily feel it was the actor's place to know anything beyond what was in the script. Hitch was famous for saying, "Actors are cattle," a claim he later corrected: "I didn't say actors were cattle. I said actors should be treated like cattle." Hitchcock was joking, of course. The extraordinary and deep performances he got not only from Montgomery Clift, but from all his actors prove that he, without perhaps a more conventional way of communicating with his actors, knew how it would all cut together.

Most of Hitchcock's wrong men are glamorous—even Monty Clift in his priest's robes still retains his striking good looks. There's a deliberate attempt to keep the wrong man on the side of the audience. Cary Grant's characters in *North by Northwest* and *To Catch a Thief* are the best illustrations of wrong men with a touch of class.

But in the late fifties, with the arrival of the French New Wave cinema and in America independent films such as *Easy Rider* (1969), audiences began to appreciate edgy, deglamorized heroes. Free of many of the restrictions imposed by censorship, Hitchcock could also embrace a new portrayal of his wrong man—and he did so in *Frenzy* (1972).

Frenzy was a difficult shoot. Alma had recently suffered a stroke and Hitch was no longer a young man. Knowing the pressure, the hours, the logistics involved with making a film, particularly on location, one can appreciate Hitchcock's courage and determination. The same qualities apply to Richard Blaney, the wrong man in *Frenzy*, portrayed by Jon Finch. He is accused of strangling several women, including his ex-wife, with a tie. The crimes are referred to in the tabloids as "The Necktie Murders." Blaney declaims, "In all conscience, is it likely that I would murder a woman I've been married to for ten years? . . . And rape her after ten years of marriage? Violently rape her?" The curious aspect of Blaney is that he is not really sympathetic. Of all Hitchcock's wrong men, he is probably the one we identify with least. He is unpleasant, impulsive, angry, and has no sense of humor. At one point he asks, "Do I look like a sex murderer to you? Can you imagine me creeping around London strangling all these women with ties?" The audience wants to say, "Yes." In a sense that is the strength of the film. Unlike the romantic wrong men of Hitchcock's previous films, Blaney is a realistic wrong man.

Blaney (named *Blamey* in the 1966 novel by Arthur La Bern, *Goodbye Piccadilly, Farewell Leicester Square*) is possibly the most violent of Hitchcock's wrong men. In *Saboteur*, Robert Cummings unsuccessfully tries to save the villain who is hanging on the Statue of Liberty. Guy Haines tries to strangle Bruno Anthony in *Strangers on a Train,* but only in self-defense. In *Frenzy*, Hitch made Blaney vengeful. He escapes from jail with the intention to murder Rusk, the real killer, played by Barry Foster. Arriving at Rusk's apartment with a crowbar, he enters and spots someone in

RIGHT In London on the set of *Frenzy* (1972)

bed underneath the covers. With strength and rage, Blaney beats the shape. In one of Hitchcock's most sadistic twists, a woman's arm, ringed in bracelets, falls to the side of the bed in the midst of Blaney's frenzy. Blaney pulls the bedding aside to discover that she was already dead—strangled with a necktie like all the others. In the novel, the victim is Blaney's ex-wife's secretary, and the book ends at that very ironic point. "In the movie, we have an anonymous lady whom we've never met before," said screenwriter Anthony Shaffer. "She's just another necktie murder." It could be argued that the book's ending might have been stronger because it would have further implicated Blaney since his wife's secretary had earlier reported him to the police. But the point was really to have the audience believe that it was Rusk underneath the sheets. (Both Rusk and the dead girl in the bed had red hair.) "It is true, however, that the intention with that scene was to extend to the last possible moment," Shaffer said, "the fact that the hero is in danger, that he is a loser, that he cannot win this one."

But Hitchcock decided to rescue his wrong man, too. The detective on the case, who in fact represents one of Hitchcock's most sympathetic portraits of the police force, has caught on to Rusk and arrives at the apartment to find Blaney and the dead girl. Just then, the sound of Rusk carrying something heavy (it turns out to be a trunk) up the stairs can be heard through the apartment walls. As Rusk steps in, the detective (Alec McCowen) simply says, "Mr. Rusk, you're not wearing your tie."

Jon Finch was an interesting choice for Blaney. He had just completed his role in Roman Polanski's *Macbeth* (1971), and the actor said that he thought of *Frenzy* as a low-budget film. "*Frenzy* was made for very little money," Finch said. Apparently Hitchcock simply thought Finch looked right for the part and didn't even request to watch footage from *Macbeth*, but eventually looked at it. Finch and Hitch met: "He said, 'I saw your film. You can act, that's good. Would you like to do it?' I said, yes I would. 'Okay, let's go have lunch.' And that was it. I was stunned."

Finch remembers that Hitchcock "was in command, he didn't have any problems. He was far too experienced, even though he wasn't well at the time. He was incredibly relaxed on the set." Hitch would tell Finch, "Hey, Jon, do you want to run jokes?" which is an old English way of saying, "Do you want to rehearse?" And so they would rehearse the scenes, shoot them, "and bang, you just did it like that." Finch admitted that, coming from the theater, he found the Hitchcock straight-on method a bit dispiriting, but because it was the Master, he adjusted to it and in the end said that the fact that everything was absolutely prepared to suit Hitchcock's vision "was a very good way to make a movie."

ABOVE Jon Finch as the wrong man in *Frenzy* (1972)

RIGHT On the *Frenzy* set

Prior to *Frenzy*, the last time Hitchcock had explored the theme of the wrong man had been in 1959 with *North by Northwest*. Two huge successes followed: *Psycho* (1960) and *The Birds* (1963). But afterward, Hitchcock's popularity declined. *Marnie* (1964), *Torn Curtain* (1966), and *Topaz* (1969) were not box-office hits. With *Frenzy*, Hitch was returning to the classic theme that had made him famous with *The Lodger*. Shaffer, who was asked by Hitch to write the *Frenzy* screenplay shortly after his theatrical success with the play *Sleuth*, said, "I think the public to some extent was losing confidence with the Master of Suspense. With *Frenzy*, by returning to London and to his roots, by telling a very carefully constructed old-fashioned story, this got him a big smash hit. The public responded to the film very strongly and the film put him back on the pedestal where he remains to this day."

Norman Lloyd remembers going to a private showing of *Frenzy*. After the failures of *Torn Curtain* and *Topaz*, it was obvious that with *Frenzy*, the Hitchcock touch had returned. Lloyd remembers jumping up and down with joy—and realizing that Alma was quietly crying in her seat. Like Lloyd, she knew how important *Frenzy* was to Hitchcock (and how it would connect him to his old audience and possibly to a new and young public).

John "Scottie" Ferguson in *Vertigo* (1958) is Hitchcock's most complicated wrong man. Scottie (played by James Stewart) suffers from a guilt complex. "I have acrophobia, which gives me vertigo," he says. He blames himself for the death of a fellow police officer during a rooftop chase in San Francisco and subsequently leaves the force. Not knowing what he's going to do next, he agrees to help an old college friend (played by Tom Helmore) who wants to know where his wife, Madeleine (Kim Novak), disappears to each day and why she is acting so strangely. Scottie trails her, falls in love with her, and then tries to help her face her demons, but he is unable to save her. One day, with Scottie looking on, she climbs to the top of a church bell tower and jumps off.

Vertigo is a fascinating departure from the classic Hitchcock theme of the wrong man. It is based on a French novel by Pierre Boileau and Thomas Narcejac (*From Amongst the Dead*) and is perhaps one of the master's most puzzling films in that it is atmospheric rather than suspenseful. The plot is purposely farfetched, almost dreamlike; it is a surreal rendition of the theme of the wrong man.

After Madeleine's suicide, we're witness to a trial in which the judge and the jury recognize Scottie's

ABOVE James Stewart and Kim Novak on the set of *Vertigo* (1958)

PAGE 41 Shooting exterior scenes for *Vertigo* at Mission Dolores in San Francisco

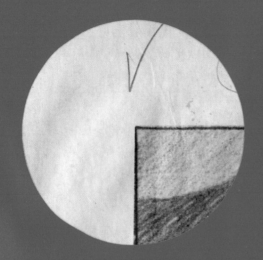

HITCHCOCK
piece by piece

innocence (he didn't kill anyone—and he did save Madeleine the first time she tried to kill herself by jumping in the San Francisco Bay), but they also accuse him of doing nothing to try to save her from her second suicide attempt ("... and justice has very little to say about things left undone"). In his heart, Scottie thinks he is responsible for Madeleine's death. He is haunted by his guilt, as he believes Madeleine was herself haunted by the ghost of one of her ancestors, a madwoman who also committed suicide. Then he meets Judy (Kim Novak, this time with dark hair), a girl who reminds him of Madeleine. In an effort to exorcise his guilt, he transforms her into Madeleine, only to discover they're one and the same. When Scottie realizes he was framed, he is no longer haunted. He understands he was blaming himself, accusing himself of something he had not done. Knowing of his acrophobia, Scottie's *friend* murdered his own wife and threw her off the bell tower. Judy, who impersonated the wife, was in on the plot.

Vertigo represents the dark, psychological side of Hitchcock's wrong men. Yet, Scottie remains one of his most romantic protagonists. James Stewart (who did four films with the master of suspense) was an unusual, yet believable, choice for the role. Stewart was perhaps more suited to playing stronger characters with a sense of humor, but he is touching and particularly good in difficult scenes where he is insisting on transforming Judy back into Madeleine. His obsession might have been laughable played by anyone else. Stewart made it seem desperately real.

The tragedy for Scottie in *Vertigo* is that in order to be free of his guilt, he needs to destroy the woman he loves and who caused his trauma. They return to the bell tower and as Judy reveals the plot, a nun steps out of a dark corner. Judy panics and falls, and this time, she is the one lying dead below. Scottie is able to look down at the body, having at once conquered his acrophobia and his guilty conscience. He is at last a free man. (The hero of the novel is not so lucky and ends up murdering the woman who betrayed him.)

Vertigo is not an easy film, and while one can understand Hitchcock's attraction to the subject matter, his approach to it was more experimental than usual. We will explore Kim Novak's performance later, but there's no doubt that the film survived the test of time because of James Stewart's portrayal of Scottie Ferguson. Stewart and Hitchcock connected on many levels, including mutual respect. Stewart always said, "You don't try to do a scene two ways. You do it one way. His." When the director passed away, Stewart, recognizing how Hitchcock had enriched his own career as an actor, declared, "I have lost a great friend, and the world has lost one of its finest directing talents. Alfred Hitchcock has made a tremendous contribution to the art of motion pictures and has been a source of joy to people all over the world."

We close the discussion on the wrong man with the most realistic of them all, because it is based on a true story, one that is spelled out literally in the title, *The Wrong Man* (1956), starring Henry Fonda. Suddenly, life is imitating fiction and Hitchcock couldn't resist, but he decided to approach the subject seriously. Instead of his usual cameo, he appeared at the beginning of the film, presenting it as fact: "In the past, I have given you many kinds of suspense pictures, but this time I would like you to see a different one. The

LEFT Henry Fonda visiting the Hitchcocks at home, 1956

difference lies in the fact that this is a true story, every word of it. And yet it contains elements that are stranger than all the fiction that has gone into many of the thrillers that I've made before."

The true story was reported in *Life* magazine (June 29, 1953) in an article written by Herbert Brean, under the title "A Case of Identity." A complete re-enactment of the case had aired on NBC, produced by Robert Montgomery (who had starred in Hitchcock's own *Mr. and Mrs. Smith,* 1941). In 1953, Manny Balestrero, a jazz bassist and father of two, was accused of stealing from an insurance company in Queens, New York. He was arrested and brought to court, but there was a mistrial because a juror spoke out from the jury box. Luckily, and almost by pure coincidence, the real guy pulled another robbery and was arrested. Manny

was cleared of all charges, but the events led his wife close to the edge of madness.

The Wrong Man is probably one of Hitchcock's most humanistic films. In it, you feel the madness slowly overtaking the wife (Vera Miles), her hope slipping away at the realization that life is cruel. This story has no humor. The events are tragic, not manipulated to be entertaining, which makes the film an anomaly in the director's body of work. But it does show most starkly Hitchcock's preoccupation with justice in an unfair world. At one point, Manny Balestrero shouts out, "Don't you see I'm just trying to tell the truth?" More than any other of Hitchcock's wrong men, Manny keeps claiming his innocence.

Hitchcock's wild imagination is obvious in *North by Northwest, The 39 Steps, Young and Innocent,* and

To Catch a Thief. These films are pure entertainment despite the darkness of the backdrop. In *The Wrong Man*, Hitchcock shifted his focus from fanciful thrills to gritty realism. He met with the judge who tried the original case, William B. Groat, who confirmed that on April 21, 1953 a member of the jury made the mistake of calling out from the box, "Do we have to sit here and listen to this?" resulting in the mistrial. Then Hitchcock visited the places where the events took place and incorporated them in his depiction of the story. As a result, *The Wrong Man* has a documentary feel to it despite Hitchcock's stylized visuals, including his use of black and white, shadows, and a film-noir atmosphere. When Manny is arrested, we follow all of the steps involved with putting a man in jail. But maybe Hitchcock went too far in his commitment to the truth? He was famous for saying that movies were like life with the dull bits cut out.

In this case, we get a blow-by-blow description of a man's slow descent into hell for a crime he didn't commit. Henry Fonda is masterful in his portrayal of Manny. In his most touching scenes, he tucks his son in bed and says, "I hope you never have to go through anything like I did. And if you ever do, I hope you got a son just like I do to come back to." But Hitchcock seems to have forgotten to be entertaining. *The Wrong Man* lacks suspense. Hitchcock focused on the emotional core of the story, and you can certainly applaud him for that choice. Even today the film may disappoint, despite its courageous approach. But considered as part of Hitch's Wrong Man canon, it stands out as clearly defining the filmmaker's stand on the subject.

Although the film doesn't have the usual Hitchcockian humorous touches, there's a certain irony when a policeman says to Manny, "An innocent man

LEFT All eyes are on Robert Montgomery as Hitchcock, seated in front of the desk, directs him on the set of *Mr. & Mrs. Smith* (1941)

ABOVE Hitchcock, Mary Clare, and a boy on the set of *Young and Innocent* (1937)

has nothing to fear. Remember that." At that point, the audience may be tempted to scream back at the screen, "Hey, haven't you seen any of Hitchcock's films?"

To understand Alfred Hitchcock, the man himself, you have to turn to his wife, Alma Reville, rather than to his protagonists. In real life, Alfred Hitchcock apparently hated the unexpected. "When I gave birth to our only child, Pat," Alma said, "I had a relatively easy time of it, but Hitch suffered such panic pains, he might as well have changed places with me!" He was very orderly, meticulous, and very well organized. "People who worked with Hitch describe him as the placid, nerveless type, but they don't realize that beneath his cherubic-like surface there is a deep pool of emotion." That pool of emotion is present in several of his leading men.

While we've seen how Hitchcock offered many variations on the wrong man, he also presented other types of leading men. One of them is the lead of *Foreign Correspondent*, Johnny Jones (played by the fantastic Joel McCrea), who is best summarized (at least at the beginning of the film) in his own words: "I'm just as big a jackass as I ever was. Bigger!" Jones, a reporter sent to Europe, unexpectedly finds himself chasing a group of enemy agents. They have faked the assassination of a Dutch diplomat and kidnapped him in the hope that he will reveal a secret that could stop the outbreak of World War II.

Foreign Correspondent's script (nominated for an Academy Award) was by Charles Bennett and Joan Harrison, with help from James Hilton for the dialogue and Robert Benchley, who appeared in the film and wrote some of its most humorous lines. It is based on a best-seller called *Personal History*. The producer Walter Wanger had tried to get the project off the ground for several years, and only when the threat from Germany emerged did the movie become a reality. Wanger negotiated with Selznick to hire Hitchcock, who was immediately attracted to the subject matter and to the setting. (Although the film was shot in Hollywood, it took place in Europe and England.) Joel McCrea's natural good looks combined with a sort of clumsiness made him ideal as Johnny Jones, an American reporter abroad on his first international assignment.

In the film, the hero's biggest dilemma is not the impending war—it's the fact that he has fallen in love with Carol Fisher (played by Laraine Day), the daughter of Stephen Fisher (played by Herbert Marshall, who had appeared in Hitchcock's *Murder!* in England), a man McCrea's Jones knows to be a

ABOVE With Joel McCrea on the set of *Foreign Correspondent* (1940)

RIGHT At home with Alma Reville, 1974

traitor. She's unaware of her father's activities and things get very complicated when she discovers that indeed Johnny is right.

Foreign Correspondent does contain one of the most memorable love declarations of all of Hitch's films: Johnny says to Carol, "I love you and I want to marry you." She answers, "I love you and I want to marry you." To which he replies, "That narrows things quite a bit, doesn't it." And so the "jackass" from the opening of the film is transformed by love. As Johnny says, "It's made a new man out of me."

For *Notorious* (1946), Hitchcock chose Cary Grant to play the role of Devlin, a government agent who falls in love with Alicia (Ingrid Bergman), the daughter of an American traitor. Rather than the somewhat goofy characters he would portray in *North by North-*

west and *To Catch a Thief,* or had portrayed in *Suspicion,* Grant plays a serious role in *Notorious,* which capitalized on his finest qualities. As Agent Devlin, Grant is truly a star: elegant, sexy, and strong.

Hitchcock would have a similar approach with John Gavin in *Psycho,* Rod Taylor in *The Birds,* Sean Connery in *Marnie,* Paul Newman in *Torn Curtain,* and Frederick Stafford in *Topaz.* They play the strong, silent type: nurturing, protective, and romantic while maintaining a composed façade.

Rod Taylor got on famously with Hitchcock, unlike Paul Newman, who was a Method actor like Montgomery Clift. Taylor in *The Birds* and Sean Connery in *Marnie* fit well in the director's frame of mind, but most importantly, in his literal movie frame. You could bring as much as you wanted to the part as long as you stayed within the frame, the

ABOVE Hitchcock directing Rod Taylor and Suzanne Pleshette on the set of *The Birds* (1963)
RIGHT With Sean Connery on the set of *Marnie* (1964)

design of the shot. Taylor recalls getting a call out of the blue to meet with Hitchcock. "I was a brash young brat," the actor said, "and I didn't say all the right things. I said something like, 'I hope the birds don't overshadow the characters in the story.' But eventually, the discussion went in another direction—and we just talked about making movies and I told him how much I loved his work. And that was it. We didn't go into any deep discussions about *The Birds*, about what we thought of Mitch, the character I played. I wanted to work with him, and I was astonished that he wouldn't mind working with 'the kid.'"

Sean Connery had a similar connection with the director: "I had a great time with Hitchcock. He tells you on the set what moves he wants. The only major direction he gave me was when I was listening to what

somebody else was saying in a scene, and he pointed out that I was listening with my mouth open—as I often do—and he thought it would look better shut."

In a sense, the best relationships Hitchcock had with his actors may have been when they looked up to him and knew how important it was to play by his rules—not because they had to, but because he knew better. It was a matter of trust, particularly later in his career when his success and influence in the business couldn't be ignored. Nevertheless, not all actors fell under Hitch's sway. Paul Newman, like Monty Clift, proved to be more skeptical about Hitchcock's approach. In *Torn Curtain*, Newman plays Professor Michael Armstrong, a scientist who pretends to defect to the East, but is in fact after a formula he is hoping to return to America. Even his

girlfriend (played by Julie Andrews) is unaware that Michael's defection is an act. Hitchcock got the idea for *Torn Curtain* when he heard the true story of two British diplomats, Guy Burgess and Donald MacLean, who had defected to Russia. Hitch wondered, "What did Mrs. MacLean think of the whole thing?"

Torn Curtain is about the average man playing spy games. Along the way, he has to lie, commit murder, and cheat in order to steal the formula. What fascinated Hitchcock about the character was his duality: he was a hero in his own country but a villain in enemy country. At the beginning, we're not even sure which side he is on. The script was written by novelist Brian Moore, with uncredited dialogue re-writes by Keith Waterhouse and Willis Hall. For the female lead, Hitch hired Julie Andrews, then already famous for her Oscar-winning title role in *Mary Poppins* (1964), *The Sound of Music* (1965), and her illustrious stage career. The situation was typical Hitchcock, but the script was simply not up to his usual standards. Before shooting started on August 30, 1965, Newman let Hitchcock know that he had problems with the script and sent him a detailed memo, which opened on a friendly note: "My son is a trampoline expert, as you may or may not know, and he taught me to do a front and back flip off the diving board. As a result, I am writing a novel entitled, 'I flipped at forty.' Well, to the work . . . " Newman went on to raise fourteen specific issues he had with the script, some relating to credibility, some to the characterization of his role. Newman also objected to the title, which he felt lacked the mystery that titles like *Notorious* and *North by Northwest* had.

Right or wrong, this memo was probably not well received by the director. "The most important

thing is to get the actor to look in the right direction," Hitch said. "If you've got a Method actor, you're in trouble, because he'll only look where he feels." Hitch once said he used to envy Walt Disney because if he didn't like one of his actors, he could just tear it up! Hitch likened actors to children. "They need to be petted and guided and should be patted on the head. Occasionally, they need a good spanking too." Years after *Torn Curtain*, Paul Newman said, "I think I could have hit it off with Hitchcock if the script had been better. It was not a lack of communication or a lack of respect. The only thing that constantly stood in our way was the script."

Mark Rutland, another deep-pool-of-emotion hero, falls in love with *Marnie* (Tippi Hedren) the minute he sees her. Played by Sean Connery, Rutland recognizes her as a compulsive thief practically on sight, but in a sort of sick game decides to ignore that particular character flaw when she is hired by his father's company. Indeed, even though Marnie is a self-declared "cheat, liar, and a thief," Mark is intrigued by her. He studies animal instincts and behavior and believes he has found his prized subject in Marnie. His intentions are not all so pure. Marnie is the way she is because of a childhood trauma, one Mark wants to understand.

The casting of Sean Connery was essential and is the reason why we, as the audience, can accept Mark's behavior. Unlike many of Hitchcock's leading men, he is forceful, violent. He even at one point rapes Marnie, although, it must be said, the scene is shot with great taste and cinematic style in a way that leaves us perplexed rather than shocked and offended. At that point in time, Sean Connery had just done a splash in

Dr. No (1962). In people's minds, he was James Bond. And his behavior as Mark Rutland in *Marnie* is not all that different from his behavior towards women as Bond. "How Sean got the part was very funny," screenwriter Jay Presson Allen revealed. "We'd been talking about a lot of different leading men, and Hitch mentioned Sean Connery. We screened scenes from *Dr. No*, and Hitch and I laughed when we thought, 'Here we are casting Sean Connery to play the part of a young man from Philadelphia for *Marnie*.' But we said, 'Let's do it!'" And so they did.

Allen remembers, too, that on the set Sean Connery was very popular with everyone, but because of his working class background, he could relate to the crew. "Sean had a very expensive watch," *Marnie*'s screenwriter recalled. "The guys on the set wanted to thank him at the end of the film, and they all gathered some money and got a watch that was not of the class he had on. Yet, Sean took it, disposed of the one he had on, and wore the one that the guys had gotten for him. That was typical Sean."

In 1953, Lew Wasserman, head of the talent agency MCA, got his client Alfred Hitchcock a lucrative deal with Paramount. One of the most important figures in Hitchcock's career, and by all accounts, a "hero" of the film industry, Wasserman secured as part of the arrangement Hitch's ownership of the rights to several of his films. The first one was immediately hailed as a classic, *Rear Window* (1954), based on a short story by Cornell Woolrich (also known as William Irish). The concept, a man who can't leave his home, starts observing his neighbors, and becomes convinced that one of them murdered his wife, immediately appealed

to the director. For the script, Hitchcock turned to John Michael Hayes, who wrote radio scripts before moving on to film and was also represented by MCA. After *Rear Window,* Hitch asked him to write his next three films, *To Catch a Thief* (1955), *The Trouble with Harry* (1955), and the remake of *The Man Who Knew Too Much* (1956).

After reading the script, James Stewart immediately committed to playing the lead, L.B. Jefferies, a news photographer who got too close to the action (taking photos at a car race) and finds himself stuck in his New York apartment with one leg in a cast (a prisoner in "a plaster cocoon," as Jefferies likes to describe his condition).

In *Rear Window*, Stewart would play yet another type of male protagonist for Hitchcock: a man who is afraid of commitment. Specifically, Jefferies refuses to marry the gorgeous Lisa Fremont (Grace Kelly) because (he claims) she is too perfect. While waiting for his leg to heal, he thinks a murder has been committed. In his effort to discover if his neighbor across the way indeed killed his wife, Jefferies takes a personal journey, during which he discovers that he does need a woman and that, having witnessed the worse type of marriage across the courtyard from his rear window vantage point, he may just be ready to recognize true love.

Rear Window is a tense suspense thriller, but also a satire on male stubbornness, exemplified by men like Jefferies who think that they're being truthful about not wanting to get married when in fact they're in denial about their feelings. Hitchcock slyly sets the tone at the beginning of the film, when a man on the radio playing in Jefferies's apartment says, "Men, are

LEFT On the set of *Rear Window* (1954)

ABOVE With James Stewart as L.B. Jefferies

you over forty? When you wake up in the morning, do you feel tired, run-down? Do you have that restless feeling?" As Jefferies stares out his rear-view window contemplating his life, his neighbor's lives are on full display. There's a heat wave; the curtains are pulled back and the windows thrown wide open. Jefferies witnesses a full range of domestic trials, including a young married couple who, over the course of the film, begin to bicker when the husband admits that he doesn't have a job; an unmarried, unsuccessful songwriter; a woman they nicknamed Miss Lonelyhearts and another referred to as Miss Torso; and the mysterious, would-be wife-killer Lars Thorwald (played by Raymond Burr). As brilliantly observed by critic Robin Wood, with *Rear Window* Hitchcock imprisons us with his protagonist—we follow the story exclusively from his point of view. More than in any other Hitchcock film, we are forced to be part of the story.

And of course, one can't neglect the amazing performance by James Stewart. As Norman Lloyd pointed out, "For an American audience, Jimmy Stewart was them. He was the guy sitting in the seat. Cary Grant was more of an aristocratic world, a drawing room world, a rich world. You aspired to his world, but you weren't in it. With Stewart, you were in his world. He came from a modest background and carried that into most of his films. He had an everyman quality about himself."

Alfred Hitchcock was 75 when he made his last film, *Family Plot* (1976), based on *The Rainbird Pattern,* a novel by Victor Canning, adapted by his *North by Northwest* screenwriter, Ernest Lehman. For this last film, Hitchcock decided to leave us with yet another

average man—George Lumley, played by Bruce Dern. He is neither a wrong man, nor a voyeur, nor someone struggling with deep issues. He is a starving actor who works as a taxi driver and thinks he'll make fast money by helping his pseudo-psychic girlfriend Blanche (Barbara Harris) find the heir to the Rainbird family fortune. Both George and Blanche get more than they bargained for when they discover that the heir is actually a criminal. The book was a crime novel. But Hitchcock turned it into much more a macabre tale with a lot of humor, mainly delivered through the dynamics of the George-Blanche duo. Their exchanges are full of sexual innuendos and great fun. *Family Plot* was Bruce Dern's second film with Hitchcock—he had a small part in *Marnie* as the sailor she kills. In the years following that first appearance, Dern made sure he was cast in several episodes of the Alfred Hitchcock television show. When *Family Plot* came about, it is Dern's belief that he got the part because Hitchcock and Universal wanted to make the film for a low budget—and not pay the enormous amount of money they'd given to both Julie Andrews and Paul Newman

LEFT On the set of *Family Plot* (1976)

ABOVE Bruce Dern in a scene from *Family Plot*

for *Torn Curtain*. When Bruce Dern went to meet with Hitchcock about the part, the actor asked the director why he had chosen him over other inexpensive actors. "Bruce, I never know what you're going to do next," Hitchcock answered. It is surprising that at the end of his career, Hitchcock, who was known for not wanting any surprises, particularly from his actors, was attracted to someone like Bruce Dern. And indeed, his portrayal of George appears favorably playful and free. But let's be clear: Bruce Dern knew he had to stay within Hitchcock's frame, figuratively and literally.

But there's one protagonist who appears in practically all of Hitchcock's films. Alfred Hitchcock himself! At the beginning of each of his films, the logical question would be, "Mr. Hitchcock, where will you appear in the film?" With the tradition established,

audiences looked for the cameos, so Hitchcock tried to appear as early as possible. He wanted his public to concentrate on the plot, not on spotting him. When *Family Plot* came about, however, Hitchcock simply wouldn't settle on where he was going to appear. His producer, Howard Kazanjian, made suggestions, but the director vetoed them. Hitchcock confided to Dern that he was thinking about not having a cameo in the film. Dern said, "Oh God, you got to have an appearance." To which the director replied, "What about I do and don't?" And that's exactly what happened. At one point, Dern's character goes to the office of Vital Statistics, and you see Hitchcock's silhouette through a glass door talking to a woman (an extra). Hitchcock is neither a wrong man nor a villain. He is the director himself! Hitchcock was the real hero of his own films.

ABOVE Hitchcock's cameo appearance in *Family Plot* (1976)

PAGE 57 At home in Bel Air, California, 1974

HITCHCOCK
piece by piece

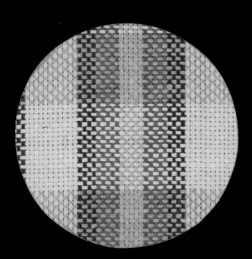

HITCHCOCK
piece by piece

the hitchcock women

CHAPTER II

Blondes, brunettes, and mothers,
but mainly blondes

"The typical American woman is a tease—dresses for sex and doesn't give it," Hitchcock said. "A man puts his hand on her, and she runs screaming for Mother. English women are the opposite—outwardly cool, but, boy, underneath!"

Women played an important role in Hitchcock's life and career. His wife, Alma Reville, was at his side in all aspects of his life and work, and his daughter, Pat (who subsequently had three daughters of her own, Mary, Katie, and Tere), worked as an actress for him and is still carrying on her father's legacy. But there were others:

Peggy Robertson, Hitch's personal assistant, who started on *Under Capricorn* (1949) and stayed with Hitch until his last film, *Family Plot* (1976).

Joan Harrison, a trusted collaborator who moved with the Hitchcocks to America. Harrison co-wrote *Jamaica Inn* (1939), *Rebecca* (1940), *Foreign Correspondent* (1940), *Suspicion* (1941), and *Saboteur* (1942). She also worked closely on the Alfred Hitchcock television shows.

Hitchcock worked with three other women screenwriters, aside from his wife and Joan Harrison. They were Dorothy Parker (on *Saboteur*), Sally Benson (*Shadow of a Doubt*, 1943), and Jay Presson Allen (*Marnie*, 1964).

There was Edith Head, the costume designer who brought glamour and substance to Hitchcock's actors through her understanding that wardrobe could reveal character. They collaborated for the first time in 1946 on *Notorious* and continued to work together on most of the master's best films, until *Family Plot*.

But, aside from his wife, perhaps the director's most important collaborators on his films were his actresses. No one can reflect on a Hitchcock film without thinking about Grace Kelly, Tippi Hedren, Janet Leigh, Ingrid Bergman, Joan Fontaine, Doris Day, Kim Novak, Eva Marie Saint, and others. Blondes or brunettes, women were an integral component of the complex universe of Hitchcock's films, but mostly they were blondes.

One hardly thinks immediately of a Hitchcock film as having anything to do with love. In fact, most of his plots have everything to do with it. A good illustration of this can be found in *Spellbound* (1945). Ingrid Bergman tracks down Gregory Peck at a hotel where he has gone to hide because he is suspected of being a killer. She believes he is innocent and wants to help—but she has also fallen in love with him. Embracing him, she says, "I am here as a doctor. . . . It has nothing to do with love!" This contradiction shows how complex Hitchcock's characters were and how crucial the love equation is in understanding his films. The mysteries are often an excuse for bringing men and women together.

Hitch and his wife met when he was "an editorial errand boy told by everybody to keep out of the way," the director said. "She was already a cutter and producer's assistant and seemed a trifle snooty to me. I couldn't notice Alma without resenting her." This situation seemed to have somewhat inspired the encounters between men and women in several of his films. On first meeting, one of the two resents the other, yet the attraction is there.

Following the initial encounters of his male and female leads, Hitchcock's approach to seduction and sex is equally considered. "My attitude toward sex is the same as it is toward other aspects of my work," the

RIGHT With costume designer Edith Head on the set of *Family Plot* (1976)

director said. "Understatement all the time. I'm not a believer in hanging sex all over a woman. It should be discovered in the course of the story." His scenes of seduction are playful, sensual, and, yes, suspenseful. And how did Hitchcock himself declare his love to Alma? "The day I proposed marriage to Alma, she was lying in an upper bunk of a ship's cabin," the director recalled on several occasions. "The ship was floundering in a most desperate way, and so was Alma, who was sick. . . . As it was, she groaned, nodded her head, and burped. It was one of my greatest scenes—a little weak on dialogue, perhaps, but beautifully staged and not overplayed." Hitch took the burp as a *yes,* and the couple was married on December 2, 1926. "I had wanted to become first a movie director and, second, Alma's husband," Hitchcock said.

When Alfred Hitchcock received the Life Achievement Award from the American Film Institute in 1979, he said, "Four people have given me the most affection, appreciation and encouragement, and constant collaboration. The first of the four is a film editor. The second is a scriptwriter. The third is the mother of my daughter, Pat, and the fourth is as fine a cook as ever performed miracles in a domestic kitchen. Their names are Alma Reville." The simplicity of their relationship and domestic life was certainly not reflected in Hitchcock's films. For the most part, marriage, or the idea of it, was very complicated. And that complication was brought in by women.

Grace Kelly is probably Hitchcock's most iconic blonde. In her first film for Hitchcock she played a role that was usually played by men: she was a "wrong woman," accused of murder in *Dial M for Murder*

(1954). The film was based on a hit play by Frederick Knott. Although Hitchcock liked to say he "called that one in," *Dial M for Murder* is a classic suspense thriller in which Tony Wendice (Ray Milland) arranges the murder of his adulterous wife, Margot (Grace Kelly). But when the killer strikes, attempting to strangle his victim, Margot grabs a pair of scissors and stabs the man in the back (a scene reminiscent of *Blackmail*, in which Anny Ondra stabs a man who is trying to rape her). You think Margot is lucky to have escaped murder, but things turn against her when her liaison with Mark Halliday (Robert Cummings) surfaces. The husband makes it look like the killer was blackmailing Margot. She loses the sympathy of the jury and is condemned to death for murder. The inspector in charge (John Williams) is skeptical, however, and manages to prove Margot's innocence with Mark's help. What is memorable about Grace Kelly in the film is her transformation. She goes from glamorous and sexy to vulnerable and defeated. Hitchcock did a masterful job making a seemingly unsympathetic character (she is, after all, cheating on her husband) completely sympathetic. The audience roots for her even before we find out the husband's murderous intentions. With Grace Kelly, Hitchcock had truly found the perfect leading lady. She had sex appeal on the surface, but a near-childlike mischievousness underneath.

"They [the studios] all said at first she was too cold, sexless," Hitchcock once recalled. "But to me she always was, and still is, a snow-covered volcano." And specifically about her performance in *Dial M*, he said, "Remember Grace Kelly in *High Noon*? She was rather mousy. But in *Dial M for Murder*, she blossomed out for me splendidly, because the touch of elegance had always been there."

LEFT Alfred and Alma's wedding, December 2, 1926

The opening sequences of *Dial M for Murder* reveal her adultery with no dialogue, just a few cuts, but they give us an immediate take on Grace Kelly's range. It's morning. Tony Wendice and Margot are having breakfast. She is reading the newspaper. She looks over the pages to make sure the husband is not noticing her sudden joy. We cut to an item in the paper announcing that famous mystery novelist Mark Halliday is coming to town. We see the ship arriving and cut to an embrace and deep kiss between Margot (purposely dressed in a red) and Mark. They catch their breath, and Margot announces, "Tony has changed . . ."

Dial M for Murder stands out because, aside from the fact that it was shot in 3D (!), it casts the glamorous Kelly in an unglamorous role, yet, she never ceases to be compelling. Hitchcock knew what he had. For instance, he decided to reveal the progression of the trial by staying almost exclusively on her. The trial remains off-screen. There's not even a set, just Kelly's reactions to the soundtrack of accusations and the devastating judgment. At the end, when her husband is finally caught, she turns away and cries. In that instant, she conveys her complicity in what happened. She blindly married a man who was only interested in her money—and she nearly paid the highest price for her mistake.

Marriage and seduction are center stage in Kelly's two other star turns for Hitch, *Rear Window* (1954) and *To Catch a Thief* (1955). You can experience *Rear Window* as a thriller—a man with a broken leg who believes a neighbor was murdered. But as seen through Kelly's performance, the film is about seduction, love, and marriage. James Stewart (L.B.

Jefferies) is a man married to his career as a news photographer. Grace Kelly (Lisa Fremont) is in love with him, but she is the glamorous type. She wears the latest fashion (as Jefferies mentions, she is the type who never wears the same dress twice), goes to social events, and wants Jefferies to have that life, too. She'll do anything to win him over—and her scenes of seduction are not only sexy but also funny. Hitchcock taps into the actress's humorous side, and she plays the part with pitch-perfect, light-hearted sex appeal. Unlike the vulnerable role she played in *Dial M for Murder*, she will stop at nothing to get her man. And as she declares, when she wants a man, she wants *all of him*. The most seductive aspect of her personality is her own knowledge that she is attractive. When she displays her nightgown, she says, "Preview of coming attractions." But Jefferies is not convinced that marriage is in the cards for him and Lisa. Is he simply afraid of marriage? Kelly's role in the film is to change Jefferies's mind. Their love game is in fact a bigger mystery than the murder case happening across the way, and Hitchcock cleverly uses the plot to help resolve the relationship between Lisa and Jefferies.

The role of marriage in *Rear Window* can't be explored without mentioning the pivotal influence of Stella, played by the hilarious character actress Thelma Ritter. She comes to give massages to Jefferies and is full of practical wisdom and reason. Her dialogue alone is a handbook to marriage—à la Hitchcock, of course—it's humorous, but also cunningly reveals the heart of the story:

She believes that every man is ready for marriage when the right girl comes along, and that "Lisa Fremont is the right girl for any man with half a brain and who can get one eye open."

RIGHT Grace Kelly and James Stewart relaxing on the set of *Rear Window* (1954)

She doesn't claim to be an educated woman, but she thinks that when a man and a woman see each other and like each other, "They ought to come together, *wham!* Like a couple of taxis on Broadway. . . . Not sit around analyzing each other like two specimens in a bottle."

Above all, she deplores the modern world's approach to love. "Now, it's read a lot of books, fence a lot of four-syllable words, psychoanalyze each other until you can't tell the difference between a party and a civil service exam."

She prefers the simpler route. "I've got two words of advice for you: marry her!"

With Stella and Lisa working together, Jefferies doesn't stand a chance. In fact, by the end of the movie, he can't stand at all. He breaks his other leg falling out of the window when the killer tries to silence him. Still there's no doubt he'll be standing at the altar as soon as he can.

To Catch a Thief is similar to *Rear Window* in that, on the surface, the main concern seems to be about solving the mystery: who is the cat burglar who is robbing the rich on the French Riviera? In fact, the real story is whether Grace Kelly is going to catch not a thief, but a man—in this case, Cary Grant. Kelly's character's approach here is different, however. She plays it cool. In one scene she seems to ignore Grant as he escorts her to her hotel room until she turns around, kisses him passionately, and then closes the door in his face. Later, during fireworks, Kelly makes a pass at Grant again. This time, she is wearing a gorgeous necklace, and she tempts him with it. "Look . . . diamonds. Hold them," she tells him. "They're the

ABOVE Hitchcock, Grace Kelly, and Alma Reville on the set of *To Catch a Thief* (1955)

RIGHT With Cary Grant and Grace Kelly

most beautiful thing in the whole world, and the one thing you can't resist." When Grant's character (a former jewel thief) tells her that they both know the necklace is fake, Kelly responds, "But I'm not." The passionate kissing that follows, intercut, as it is, with shots of fireworks exploding above the Côte D'Azur, is symbolically obvious.

In *To Catch a Thief*, Cary Grant and Grace Kelly do make an attractive duo—and play up the comic banter well. Since Kelly's character Frances Stevens is introduced as a frigid young woman and Grant's John Robie is introduced as a loner, the real tension of the film lies in whether they will come together. Yes, it's important for Grant to catch the real thief, the copycat who is pinning jewel thefts on him, but it's more important for him to have Kelly believe that

he is innocent, a reformed man. Kelly's motivations are vaguer, yet just as compelling. She goes back and forth between being attracted to the danger (it feels like she almost wants Robie to be guilty so she can add his infamous name to her list of conquests) and being repulsed by him (particularly when she believes that he has stolen her mother's jewels). Amid this ambivalence, Frances also exhibits flashes of jealousy of Robie's previous women as well as those who might be her current competition, such as the young woman played by French actress Brigitte Auber. In *To Catch a Thief*, Kelly plays a woman unsure of her desires, but by the end of the film, having discovered that Robie is in fact innocent, she knows that she is ready for marriage. Even more important, just as she convinced James Stewart's character in *Rear Win-*

dow that he needed her, she manages to make Robie admit that he "can't just do everything" by himself; that he "needed the help of a good woman"; and that he isn't "the lone wolf" he thought he was.

After the success of *To Catch a Thief*, it was obvious that Hitchcock wanted to continue working with Grace Kelly—and he had a role for her. Something completely different from those she had played for him so far: *Marnie*, which is almost *Spellbound* in reverse. In *Marnie*, it is the woman who is psychologically disturbed; she is helped by a man who falls in love with her. *Marnie* was slated to begin right after the success of *Psycho*. By then Grace Kelly had become the Princess of Monaco, but after discussing the possibilities with Hitch, she committed to making the film. Such strong working relationships were rare.

When the treatment by Joseph Stefano, who wrote the *Psycho* screenplay, was completed, however, Grace Kelly had changed her mind. Pat Hitchcock recalls, "Between the time she originally agreed to do the film and the time they were ready to make it, her duties in Monaco were more pressing, and Prince Rainier didn't think it was a good time for her to be gone." Hitchcock put *Marnie* aside and turned to *The Birds*. For its lead he decided to hire an actress no one had ever heard about before: Tippi Hedren.

In the early 1960s, Tippi Hedren had been modeling for over a decade, and her career was winding down. She had also done a number of television commercials. One of them ran on television frequently. Around that time the young actress found out that a director or a producer had seen the commercial, which promoted a dietary product, but she didn't know who. She received a call on October 13 (a Friday!), 1961, inviting her to Universal Studios, where she met with a studio executive. She left her headshot, but still had no idea who the mysterious director-producer interested in her acting talent was. The next step was a meeting with Herman Citron, an agent at MCA. At that point, Hedren finally learned that the filmmaker was Alfred Hitchcock, and that he wanted to sign her to a contract. It was one of those moments where she didn't know how to respond: laugh or cry? When Hedren finally met Hitch, they didn't talk about acting. Instead, they talked about food, travel, wine. He then brought in Edith Head, his trusted costume designer, and started a series of screen tests. In essence, Hitch was like the character of Scottie in *Vertigo*. He wanted to transform Hedren into the perfect actress to play one of his most intriguing blondes: Melanie Daniels in *The Birds*.

Tippi Hedren knew that there was a movie being scripted by Evan Hunter called *The Birds* (based on a novella by Daphne du Maurier), but she had no idea that she was in the running for the leading role. She thought she was being groomed for one of the *Alfred Hitchcock Presents* episodes. For her screen test, three scenes were selected: one from *Rebecca*, one from *Notorious*, one from *To Catch a Thief*, clearly a spectrum of Hitchcock leading roles: naïve and virginal (*Rebecca*), strong yet vulnerable (*Notorious*), sexy and determined (*To Catch a Thief*). Tippi learned the lines and Hitch became the drama teacher. The tests were shot by Hitch's favorite director of photography Robert Burks (who had been with him since *Strangers on a Train*), over a period of three days with actor Martin Balsam (who had just appeared as private detective Arbogast in *Psycho*) playing opposite Hedren in the tests.

RIGHT Tippi Hedren as Melanie Daniels in *The Birds* (1963)

Then Alfred and Alma Hitchcock invited her to dinner at Chasen's (one of Hollywood's most famous restaurants). With Lew Wasserman to her left and Alma and Hitch on her right, Hedren was unprepared for the surprise of her life. Hitchcock presented her with a gift box from one of his favorite shops, Gump's of San Francisco. She opened the box to find a beautiful pin of three birds in flight, decorated with seed pearls and set in gold. Hitchcock announced, "I want you to play Melanie Daniels." Hedren started crying. Then work began.

When Evan Hunter first met with Hitchcock about *The Birds*, he had already read the story by Daphne du Maurier, in which a farmer and his wife are terrorized by birds. The attacks of the birds are never explained—and Hitchcock was interested in keeping the high concept of this apocalyptic tale.

Although the story bordered on the supernatural, Hitchcock showed Hunter a series of articles about unexplained bird attacks that had occurred up and down the California coast. Hitch and Hunter met regularly and built the storyline, but then the screenwriter, with the blessing of his director, went off and wrote the script. Hitchcock gave his collaborator great freedom. He told Hunter if he wanted to have a bird coming through a keyhole, don't hesitate, put it in. Hitch said he'd take care of the rest.

In the film, Melanie Daniels, a stunning blonde, walks into a bird shop in San Francisco and meets the handsome Mitch Brenner (Rod Taylor). Melanie pretends that she works in the shop because she finds Mitch, a customer like herself, attractive. A bird gets loose, and Mitch manages to catch it. As he puts it back in the cage, he says, "Back in your gilded cage,

ABOVE Tippi Hedren during the filming of *The Birds* (1963)

Melanie Daniels," letting her know that he was on to her all along. She is a socialite whose high spirits have received at-times-unwanted public attention. He is a lawyer who has seen her in court (for a prank presumably gone slightly awry). Thus begins a game between potential lovers, who, in order to get together, will have to go through a horrendous, frightening, and inexplicable event: a massive bird attack on the small town of Bodega Bay, where Mitch retreats on weekends to be with his clinging mother (Jessica Tandy) and little sister (Veronica Cartwright). Also in the small town is a dark-haired beauty named Annie Hayworth (Suzanne Pleshette). She is the schoolteacher who moved to Bodega Bay to be near Mitch, although she knew she could never have him. Melanie has higher hopes for herself and Mitch.

With Tippi Hedren as Melanie, Hitchcock exemplified his fascination with the complexities of relationships. He throws all sorts of obstacles in Melanie's way, the biggest one being Mitch's mother, Lydia, a widow afraid of losing her son. She has already sabotaged Annie Hayworth's chances and intends to do the same with Melanie.

Unaware of what awaits her in Bodega Bay, Melanie impulsively drives there with two lovebirds, a birthday present for Mitch's sister. Intended to be a surprise, as well as an excuse to see Mitch again, Melanie's plan doesn't work out as anticipated. She is attacked by a seagull. Mitch rescues her and asks her over for dinner, but the town becomes besieged by more attacks. Melanie must fight for survival on two fronts, against the birds and against Mitch's mother's interference. When Lydia convinces Melanie to go to the school because she is afraid for her daughter, you

ABOVE Hitchcock and Tippi Hedren during the publicity tour for *The Birds* get a sense Lydia subconsciously wishes the same fate to befall Melanie as it did her neighbor, whose eyes were pecked out by birds. And Lydia nearly gets what she wishes for, but in the end, it is Melanie who conquers all. After she survives a near-fatal bird attack, the family decides to leave. One of the last shots of the film is Lydia holding Melanie against her with a smile of approval.

Tippi Hedren's performance is a complete tour de force. She immersed herself in a very difficult role in a complex film, part horror-monster movie, part psychological drama. The role, however, was no cake walk. After filming the famous scene in the upstairs bedroom where she is attacked by hundreds of birds, Hedren ended up suffering from exhaustion.

Hitchcock's meticulous design of Melanie Daniels is mesmerizing. She first appears totally in control, professional, classily dressed in black in the bird shop. Edith Head then chose a pale green outfit for her to wear for the rest of the movie, one that reflects a less rigid, more vulnerable side. And indeed, we do find out that Melanie is not only in search of a man, but also in search of a mother—hers abandoned her. "My mother? Don't waste your time," she tells Mitch. "She ditched us when I was eleven and ran off with some motel man in the East."

Another important element of the equation is Annie, Melanie's dark-haired rival. (Suzanne Pleshette had a great sense of humor and one day showed up on set wearing a blonde wig!) Annie is a self-declared open book ("... or rather a closed one," she says), who has accepted that she'd rather be near Mitch than not have him at all. Pleshette's performance is flawless, both touching and essential to the plot. She is the opposite of Melanie. She is simple,

unsophisticated, but still perceived as Melanie's rival. And she pays the price. She is killed by the birds, eliminating a potential threat to Mitch and Melanie's romance.

There is no resolution about the birds. As the Brenners and Melanie drive away, another scene was supposed to follow where the car was attacked. But in a sense, there is no end, because the conclusion of the story is a new beginning, one between Melanie and Mitch—with Lydia somewhere there in the middle.

After the success of *The Birds* (1963), it was only natural for Hitchcock to follow with another film starring his discovery, Tippi Hedren. He decided to resurrect *Marnie* (1964). At first, Hitch tried to reteam with Evan Hunter, since Joseph Stefano was now unavailable, working on his television series, *The Outer Limits*. The character of Marnie was completely different from Melanie Daniels, and one thing the two films proved was Tippi Hedren's range as an actress.

Marnie is frigid; she robs people, changes identity, and suffers from horrible nightmares. Something in her past is haunting her and is the cause of her erratic behavior. She can't stand the color red; she is frightened by thunder and lightning. The key lies in the mystery of her troubled childhood. Marnie's mother entertained men. One stormy night, the little girl killed a sailor, one of her mother's gentleman-callers who, she thought, was attacking her mother. Marnie repressed the event, but was never the same again. The story follows her recovery with the help of Mark Rutland (Sean Connery), who forces her to relive the events of that fateful night.

Evan Hunter told Hitchcock that he had a major problem with an element in the story: At one point,

PAGE 73 With Tippi Hedren on the set of *Marnie* (1964)

HITCHCOCK
piece by piece

HITCHCOCK
piece by piece

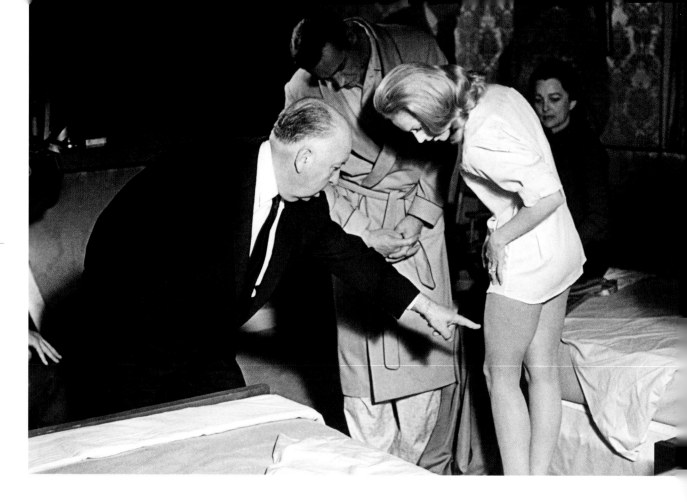

during their honeymoon, Mark Rutland forces him-self on Marnie. Hunter felt this was in essence a rape scene, and that the audience would never for-give Rutland for it. After discussing the issue with Hitchcock, Hunter understood the director did not want to abandon the scene. So Hunter wrote the script both ways, with and without the rape. As a result, Hunter was replaced by another writer, Jay Presson Allen, author of both the play and screenplay *The Prime of Miss Jean Brodie* (the film came out in 1969), based on the novel by Muriel Spark. Allen rightly felt that Connery's charisma, and Hitchcock's stylish approach to the scene, would make it work for the audience.

Louise Latham, who played Bernice, Marnie's mother, was a friend of Jay Presson Allen's; they'd gone to school together. Latham admitted she felt sorry for the character she played. She had been abandoned by Marnie's father, but she was definitely

cruel. The challenge of the role was to give Bernice a strong physical presence. She injured her leg when Marnie killed the sailor and has a limp. She also has a strong accent—and every fan of the film quotes her saying, "Marnie, mind my leg." Latham said, "One of the things I felt about her was the tightness, the physical discomfort—and not just her wounded leg, but the fact that she was uncomfortable in her body. And probably hated her body because of the past."

Like Melanie Daniels, Marnie has a dark-haired rival. Lil Mainwaring is Mark's sister-in-law; his first wife, Lil's sister, died. Lil is in love with Mark, is jealous of his affection for Marnie, and wants to bring her down. She knows there's something wrong with Marnie and hopes to win Mark by exposing it. Little does she know that Marnie's mysterious past is exactly what attracts Mark. To play Lil, Hitchcock turned to Diane Baker. She was cool, composed, and held things in. Hitchcock didn't talk about the

ABOVE With Sean Connery and Tippi Hedren during the filming of *Marnie* (1964)
RIGHT Tippi Hedren (left) and Diane Baker (right) on the *Marnie* set

character, but created on the set an environment to influence the young actress's portrayal of Lil. If he wanted her to be tense, he might pretend to ignore her during a take. Lil is fascinating. Although she is an antagonist, almost a villain in the film, Baker brings charm and innocence to her role.

In *The Birds*, Melanie Daniels wanted to get Mitch. In *Marnie*, it's the reverse. Mark wants to win Marnie over. In that sense, both films have a happy conclusion. *Marnie*, however, marks the end of an era for Hitchcock. Although the film is considered a classic by many, it wasn't well received when it first came out. *Marnie* may have appeared too stylized with its obvious process shots and painted backdrops at a time when a new generation of filmmakers was successfully bringing realism to the screen. *Marnie* would also be the last film Hitchcock would do with three of his key collaborators. Both Robert Burks (director of photography) and George Tomasini

(editor) did not work on the director's next film *Torn Curtain* (1966). Tomasini died shortly after *Marnie* and Burks was busy on other films until his death in 1968, and Hitchcock would have a falling out with his composer Bernard Herrmann over the film's score. (Herrmann wrote the score for *Torn Curtain*, but it was replaced by a new one composed by John Addison.) But above all, *Marnie* was the last collaboration between Hitchcock and the exceptional Tippi Hedren. She remains one of Hollywood's most underrated actresses.

By the time Hitchcock made his first film in America, *Rebecca* (1940), for legendary producer David O. Selznick, he had established his talent for presenting fascinating female characters. Sylvia Sidney in *Sabotage* (1936) is an unusual mix of weakness (she is dominated by a creepy terrorist of a husband portrayed by Oscar Homolka) and strength (she stabs

her husband after she finds out he was responsible for her kid brother's death). It's a remarkable scene. As Homolka approaches, sensing his wife's hesitation while she carves the meat, we hear the squeak of his shoes. We know she stabs him only by the shocked expression on his face.

There's Nova Pilbeam in *Young and Innocent* (1937) (based on the novel *A Shilling for Candles* by Josephine Tey), and Madeleine Carroll in *The 39 Steps* (1935). Both heroines fall in love with the wrong man. At first they fight their desires, but as the truth unfolds they end up recognizing the innocence of the men they love. Madeleine Carroll plays another defining Hitchcockian female role in *Secret Agent* (1936), opposite John Gielgud. They have to pretend they're married in order to unmask a German spy. Their relationship starts on the rocks—and with a

slap (literally)—but after their adventures they realize that marriage is much more attractive and far less dangerous than spying. In the final image of the film, the couple seems to be smiling at us, the audience, a device Hitchcock would use in his last film, *Family Plot*, in which Barbara Harris winks at us, breaking the fourth wall one more time in recognition of Hitchcock's great appreciation of his audience.

Rebecca is one of his greatest gifts to his audience—and it offers a unique portrayal of women in his films. For one thing, the title character never appears, but her presence dominates the film. She is both the mystery and perhaps a variation of the MacGuffin.

In the south of France, an orphaned girl working as a wealthy woman's companion (Joan Fontaine) encounters Maxim de Winter (Laurence Olivier), a rich and moody widower, on the verge of suicide. It seems he

ABOVE Madeleine Carroll and John Gielgud in *Secret Agent* (1936)
RIGHT Hitchcock and George Sanders (on the phone) in *Rebecca* (1940)

can't get over the death of his wife, Rebecca. Strangers to each other, he proposes to her, and she accepts, despite the skepticism of Mrs. Van Hopper (Florence Bates), her employer, who has been sick in bed during the hasty courtship. Max brings his "second Mrs. de Winter" home to his estate, the formidable Manderley. (The novel, written in the first person, never reveals her name and in the film, we never find out the heroine's name either.) The unsophisticated new wife is thrown into society and wealth. Even worse, at home at Manderley her days are menaced by Mrs. Danvers (Judith Anderson), the housekeeper. Mrs. Danvers remains morbidly obsessed with Rebecca and wants to destroy the woman who has presumed to take her place. It seems Mrs. Danvers might just get her way when, after a bad storm, a sunken craft is found, and Rebecca's body is discovered aboard. It

appears that at the time of Rebecca's death Maxim identified the wrong woman. By mistake or design? Could he have killed his Rebecca? In an unexpected twist, Maxim reveals to his new wife, who has had to mature quickly in order to supply Maxim with the moral support he needs, that he hated Rebecca, and that she accidentally died during a heated argument. Later, it is revealed that Rebecca had known she had cancer. It becomes clear that she wanted to die—she taunted Maxim with stories about her lovers and during the argument, she fell, killing herself, a kind of suicide after all. Mrs. Danvers would rather destroy Manderley and die than see the couple happy there. She sets the estate on fire and perishes in the flames. As the fire licks the embroidered *R* on the lace pillowcase of Rebecca's bed, it seems her ghost will no longer come between Max and his second wife.

Rebecca is a true Hitchcock film and benefits from the performance and portrayal of the second Mrs. de Winter by Joan Fontaine. "She does everything that by common agreement has come to mean girlish innocence. She does it so well that it could pass for a classroom example," declared critic Archer Winsten. But what's most remarkable is her transformation from the self-deprecating girl who says, "Every day, I realize the things that she had and that I lack; beauty and wit and intelligence and all the things that are so important in a woman," into a mature woman who can declare, "I am Mrs. de Winter now!" Her strength is reinforced when she realizes that Maxim did not love Rebecca—and that she has to be strong for him, standing by his side, as he is wrongly accused of killing his wife.

Joan Fontaine's part as Lina in *Suspicion* (1941) was in many ways similar to her role in *Rebecca*. She is at first a mousy, unsophisticated woman who blossoms by living through what she believes may be an attempt by her husband to kill her. There's an extraordinary sequence that takes place on top of a hill at the beginning of the film that sets the tone of the relationship between Lina and Johnny Aysgarth (Cary Grant). Rather than going to church, Lina has taken a walk with the seductive Johnny. The long camera shot shows them struggling, and we assume he tried to kiss her—or kill her? Suddenly the scene becomes comical; Johnny makes fun of Lina's hair and calls her "Monkey Face." The scene then turns romantic and ends with Lina closing her purse, obvious yet funny symbolism indicating her virginity. It's not until she overhears her parents discussing the prospects of her spinsterish future that Lina returns Johnny's passion. Against her parents' wishes, she marries him. Seeds of suspicion take root and grow in Lina's imagination as Johnny's lies and debt are exposed. When his best friend Beaky, a wealthy man, dies shortly before a loan to Johnny comes due, Lina's suspicion takes a dark turn. Could Johnnie be a killer? Would he stop at nothing to get himself out of debt?

ABOVE Producer David O. Selznick and Hitchcock on the set of *Rebecca* (1940)

Ultimately, like Maxim's second wife in *Rebecca*, Lina acknowledges that she has misinterpreted her husband's emotions. She admits, "This is as much my fault as yours. I was only thinking of myself, not what you were going through. If I had been really close to you, you would have confided in me, but you were afraid, ashamed to come to me." In both *Rebecca* and *Suspicion*, Joan Fontaine managed to bring extreme believability to two characters that could have appeared contrived. In the first case, "God, my husband is in love with the ghost of his first wife!" and in the second, "I fell in love with a killer!" What Joan Fontaine makes us believe, with the help of her director and co-stars, is unforgettable.

Ingrid Bergman starred in three Hitchcock films, one of which is *Notorious* (1946). In it she plays the daughter of a traitor who agrees to become an American spy and marry a Nazi living in South America in order to expose his plans. Hitchcock hired screenwriter Ben Hecht to work with him on the script and the result of their collaboration is probably one of the filmmaker's best.

As many of the master's films, *Notorious* is really a character study disguised as a thriller. It is the story of a woman feeling the heavy guilt of her father's betrayal of America. She has become an alcoholic living a louche life when she meets Devlin (Cary Grant), whose job is to enlist her in espionage. Some-

ABOVE With Gladys Cooper, Nigel Bruce, and Joan Fontaine, who starred in *Rebecca* as the second Mrs. de Winter

where along the way they fall in love. Hitchcock does a wonderful job of making the love story a crucial aspect of the plot; love is, in fact, what will save Alicia's life. When she is discovered to be an American agent, her husband, Alex Sebastian (Claude Rains), and his mother (Leopoldine Konstantin) slowly poison her. Devlin wants to believe that Alicia is just a depraved woman because she agreed to marry Alex Sebastian. But he has second thoughts. He comes to her rescue and as he carries her out of the house, it's his declaration of love that keeps her alert and moves the story to its conclusion.

Bergman is not the typical Hitchcock sexy blonde. She is subtler, more intellectual. Hitchcock uses her uniqueness to his advantage. Bergman's sophistication and European traits are what make both Grant as the good guy, and Rains, as the bad guy, fall in love with her. They're blinded by her to the point where they misread her completely. Alex doesn't realize she is a spy, and Devlin thinks she has reverted to being a drunk. And that's where the power of Bergman's performance lies—she appears weak, but is really controlling both men (consciously and subconsciously). She succeeds in the end. Sebastian will

be eliminated by his Nazi cohorts for marrying an American agent, and she gets Devlin, who confesses, "I was a fat-headed guy full of hate. I couldn't stand not having you."

The Hitchcock-Bergman harmony is obvious in both *Notorious* and *Spellbound* (1945), which they did back to back. Each film displays a completely different side of the actress, yet both characters are ready to make many sacrifices—including their own selves—for love.

Despite the fact that their next film together, *Under Capricorn* (1949), was a bit of a misfire (some kind of unofficial period remake of *Rebecca*, a hybrid version of *Notorious* and *Suspicion*, and even featuring a foreshadowing of Mrs. Bates' dead body from *Psycho* in the shape of a shrunken head used

to terrorize Ingrid Bergman) the Hitchcock-Bergman connection stayed strong. But the experience was challenging for the actress. Hitchcock was experimenting with extremely long takes (as he had with his previous film, *Rope*, 1948). It was like filmed theater. "How I hate this new technique of his," Bergman said. "How I suffer and loathe every minute on the set." On occasion, Hitchcock would remind her, "Ingrid, it's only a movie!"

There are strong echoes of Alicia in Eve Kendall, the character played by Eva Marie Saint in *North by Northwest* (1959), but only if you trace her history backward. Eve appears cold, the ultimate seductress. We initially think she is working with the villain, Phillip Vandamm, played by James Mason. She is

LEFT AND ABOVE With Ingrid Bergman on the set of *Spellbound* (1945)

later revealed to be an agent for the United States government. She confesses to Roger O. Thornhill (Cary Grant) that she fell in love with Vandamm and "saw only his charms." Later, the government approached her, told her he was a traitor, and asked her to spy on him for them, like Alicia in *Notorious*, but the reason she agreed is not completely patriotic. She is a woman who has been deceived by men—and that's her way of getting back at them. When Thornhill asks her, "What's wrong with men like me?" she replies, "They don't believe in marriage." "I've been married twice." "See what I mean?" The grand prize at the end of the film is that she's turned a man like Thornhill into the kind of marrying type he should be. In fact, it's on top of Mount Rushmore, where she is hanging by her fingernails, that he proposes. As Thornhill struggles to save her, her strength all but gone, what motivates her to persevere is his calling her "Mrs. Thornhill." Then that moment takes us directly to the famous end scene: the blonde and the wrong man, alone and happy at last, climbing up into the sleeping compartment on a train—as it suggestively enters a tunnel. *The End.*

Teresa Wright, who plays Charlie in *Shadow of a Doubt* (1943), manages to be both touching and riveting. The character of young Charlie Newton is that of a naïve girl who is bored with life. Everything is just too plain, too pretty, and too simple for young Charlie. She declares, "I guess I don't like to be an average girl in an average family." And then, with the unexpected arrival of her Uncle Charlie (her mother's brother), everything changes, but not in the way she expects.

Shadow of a Doubt was a family picture on all counts. Scenes were filmed on location in Santa Rosa, California, and the entire Hitchcock family was together on the set. As happens when film crews travel to location, everyone lived together like a big, extended family. Teresa Wright became particularly close with Pat Hitchcock. They played gin rummy during their spare time. "The thing about *Shadow of a Doubt* is that I really wanted to do it because it was Alfred Hitchcock," Teresa Wright said. "I did not read the script, but instead I was told 'he wants to tell you the script.' So I went to his office and I sat down, opposite him at a desk. And he proceeded to tell me

ABOVE With Teresa Wright on the set of *Shadow of a Doubt* (1943)
RIGHT Birthday party during the filming of *Shadow of a Doubt*

the story. And he told the story like no one else. He used props from his desk, he'd make sound effects, he'd do steps. He'd do anything that was necessary to lure you into the story. I was just mesmerized and when I saw the film completed, I said, 'I've seen this before! I saw it in his office!' And I really meant it. He was an incredible storyteller, which we know from watching his films, but he was the same in person."

Charlie, who is named after her uncle, thinks he is her hero. In fact, he is a serial killer of rich widows. The great irony about Uncle Charlie and his niece is that Hitchcock wanted them to be almost like twins. It's an actual line from the film, "But we're sort of like twins, don't you see?" the young Charlie tells her uncle. Hitch designed the interaction between the two characters along the theme of duality. "I remember when we were shooting the scene when I'm lying in bed," Teresa Wright recalled. "Hitchcock was very specific about the way he wanted to position me. And he explained why and how he wanted this to mirror the way he introduced Uncle Charlie in the film." It's almost as if Uncle Charlie could be the dark side of young Charlie's personality. We witness her transformation, her realization that the world really is as her uncle describes it, "a foul sty." But the moral of the story lies in the lesson that young Charlie learns—and the hope that Jack Graham (Macdonald Carey), her love interest, brings at the end by telling her that the world "isn't quite as bad" as she thinks but that indeed, "it needs a lot of watching."

Duality is a theme that Hitchcock explored in many of his characters, but never so literally as in *Vertigo*. Kim Novak portrays what we believe for a moment is a single actress playing two separate roles: Madeleine Elster, a haunted and suicidal woman, and Judy Barton, a plain girl from Salina, Kansas. Instead, it turns out that Kim Novak portrays one character who *pretends* to be the other. "Madeleine" is a role that Judy plays in a conspiracy to cover up the murder of the real Madeleine Elster, whom we never meet in the film. The character played by James Stewart is caught

between the two women and two worlds—fantasy and reality. The voice of reason in the film belongs, in fact, to a third woman, Midge (Barbara Bel Geddes). She is in love, unrequitedly, with Stewart's character, but she remains clear-eyed enough to know that the glamorous Madeleine is no good for him. Midge, like the character played by Diane Baker in *Marnie*, is never fully realized, but she serves as a strong contrast to the dual figures played by Kim Novak.

Another interesting aspect of Kim Novak's character in *Vertigo* is that as a blonde, she is a victim. She dies because James Stewart has recreated the image of the dead woman he thought he loved. She lets him transform her because she has fallen in love with him—but by doing so she sets herself up for the same deadly fate the real Madeleine met with.

The blonde as a victim started in *The Lodger,* and just a few years later in 1929, Hitchcock picked it up again in a jewel of a film called *Blackmail,* starring Anny Ondra. Production began as a silent movie, but when sound arrived, Hitchcock quickly had to readjust. His lead actress was Czech and spoke little English. And Hitchcock had to have another actress (Joan Barry) record the dialogue off-screen simultaneously, with Ondra pretending to talk. Unless you know that fact, the switch is seamless.

Alice White (Ondra) starts off as one of Hitchcock's strongest female characters. "It takes more than a man to frighten me!" she declares. But her confidence is soon altered when she agrees to follow a man to his house. He tries to rape her. She grabs a knife and kills him in self-defense. Her boyfriend is the detective on the case. She is then blackmailed by a stranger who saw her with the victim. Eventually the blackmailer

is killed during a chase atop the British Museum, and the detective-boyfriend convinces Alice to let people think that the blackmailer was in fact the killer. It's an ironic twist and perhaps even a life sentence (would she really want to stay with this man under normal circumstances, but what choice does she have?) for a woman who had a momentary lapse of judgment.

Many years later the consequence of impulse would be deadly for Janet Leigh. *There* is a blonde who would change the face of thrillers and cinema altogether, just by taking a shower in a creepy motel in *Psycho* (1960), which begins in a Phoenix hotel room, where Marion Crane (Janet Leigh) is spending her lunch hour with her boyfriend Sam Loomis (John Gavin). It looks like they're destined to meet that way until Sam can pay off his debts, but Marion can't wait any longer. Back at the office, in a desperate attempt to change her life and be with Sam, she steals $40,000 in cash from one of her boss's clients. With the money, Marion sets out for Fairvale, where Sam lives, but en route a rainstorm and nightfall make for difficult driving conditions. She gets lost and stops at the Bates Motel for the night. While checking in, Marion has a curious conversation with Norman Bates (Anthony Perkins), the young owner, who seems to be dominated by his mother. By this time, Marion's reason has prevailed, and she has decided to return to Phoenix to give back the money. As she steps into the shower (perhaps to wash away her guilt), she is stabbed to death by, we think, the young man's mother. Later, Marion's sister, Lila (Vera Miles), and Sam discover that the mother has been dead for many years. We find out later that it was Norman who killed her. In an attempt to expiate his guilt, he kept her body in her bedroom and occasionally im-

RIGHT With Kim Novak on the set of *Vertigo* (1958)

personated her. Each time the possibility of a woman coming between them arose, Norman took on the mother's personality and killed again.

It was the combined genius of Robert Bloch's novel, Joseph Stefano's adaptation, and Hitchcock's direction that created one of the scariest films ever made. *Psycho* revolutionized the film-going experience. Although she is killed in the first half of the film, Janet Leigh's portrayal of Marion Crane is unforgettable. Part of the twist for Hitchcock's faithful audience is that no one expected the star of the film to be killed so soon.

Hitchcock sent the novel *Psycho* by Robert Bloch to Janet Leigh with a note explaining that the script would be different. "Hitchcock wanted me to know that Marion would not be quite the description in the novel, but it was important to him that I got a feeling for the character and that I realized it was a short part," Leigh explained. The actress read the book, loved it, and met the director at his home. He showed her models of every set. He had a miniature camera and explained how he visualized each shot.

Hitchcock explained to Janet Leigh that *Psycho* was a pie. And that he had a slice of it for her. "He told me, 'You're a professional,'" Janet Leigh said, "'I really won't direct you unless you're having problems. I won't interfere with your interpretation unless you take more than your slice of the pie...'" As an actress, Janet Leigh was liberated by the director's work ethic. "It seems to me he was giving the actor the greatest compliment he could possibly give!"

And the actress didn't mind that her character was being killed off so fast—she knew Marion Crane was important and the fact that an established star played the role doubled the impact. Janet Leigh recalled, "After the film came out, people kept telling me how they thought I would somehow reappear in the film, even though I was dead!"

Janet Leigh's murder in the shower has become a textbook example of filmmaking. It was shocking at the time and remains today one of the greatest moments of cinema ever created. But it has at its center Janet Leigh's devastating performance as she slides down against the shower wall, grabs the curtain, and falls head-first on the bathroom floor—followed by the swirling of blood and water down the drain, then dissolving to her dead stare. This sequence alone has inspired many generations of filmmakers.

Vera Miles as Lila is even tougher than Marion. She breaks laws without remorse in order to discover what happened to her sister. This is an entirely different character from Rose, whom she played in *The Wrong Man* (1956). In that film Rose feels guilty for the bad luck that has befallen her family, and Miles is absolutely devastating as she spirals down, eventually, into madness. Miles's range from *The Wrong Man* to *Psycho* makes it obvious why Hitchcock liked the actress so much. She would have made a great Madeleine/Judy in *Vertigo*, a role intended for her, but she became pregnant and had to decline.

LEFT With Janet Leigh on the set of *Psycho* (1960)

ABOVE Henry Fonda and Vera Miles in *The Wrong Man* (1956)

The other interesting female character in *Psycho* is Pat Hitchcock, the director's daughter in her third and last screen role for him. She plays, with great humor and ease, Carolyn, Marion's co-worker. Although it is a small part, she completely ties in with the themes of the movie: marriage and matriarchal dominance. When the boss's client flirts with Marion, Carolyn is quick to say, "He must have noticed my wedding ring." Later, listing the calls that came in while Marion was out, she says, "Teddy [her husband] called me—my mother called to see if Teddy called." And when Marion complains of a headache, Carolyn says, "I've got something. Not aspirin—my mother's doctor gave them to me the day of my wedding." In her previous roles for her father, Pat Hitchcock was also the comic relief. In *Stage Fright* (1950), she was Chubby Banister, a friend of Eve Gill (Jane Wyman). She only has a few lines but is hilarious. She had a much bigger part in *Strangers on a Train* (1951), as the sister of Ruth Roman, Farley Granger's girlfriend, another comical role, always speaking her mind at the most inopportune times.

It's no surprise that Pat Hitchcock had a talent for comedic roles. Humor was one of her father's trademarks, and he had quite a few funny female characters in his films. There was of course one of the Hitchcock family's favorites, Carole Lombard, who starred in *Mr. and Mrs. Smith* (1941). Shirley MacLaine plays the wife of Harry, who is dead, in *The Trouble with*

Harry (1955). She is adorable and plays in this dark comedy with great ease. At one point she says, "Frankly, I don't care what you do with Harry just as long as you don't bring him back to life!" Few actresses could deliver such a line with a straight face. Another favorite funny character is Jane Wyman's

role in *Stage Fright*, a film that remains underrated. Even Hitchcock did not like the film because he felt he had made an enormous error by showing a "fake" flashback. Wyman's Eve Gill is an aspiring actress infatuated with Jonathan (Richard Todd), a man accused of killing the husband of singer-performer Charlotte Inwood (played at her evil best by Marlene Dietrich). In order to clear Jonathan's name, Eve goes undercover as a maid to Charlotte. Wyman is irresistible in her exchanges with her father (played by the wonderfully funny Alastair Sim) and her mother (Sybil Thorndike, clueless but charming). It's in disguise and while trying to make herself look ordinary

TOP Shirley MacLaine and John Forsythe in *The Trouble with Harry* (1955)
BOTTOM Jane Wyman and Hitchcock (doing his cameo appearance) in *Stage Fright* (1950)
PAGE 89 Hitchcock with his daughter, Patricia, on the set of *Strangers on a Train* (1951)

that Eve becomes extraordinary. Unwittingly, she becomes a heroine and a leading lady in a melodrama. The same goes for Madame Blanche (Barbara Harris) in *Family Plot* who, in trying to swindle some money, finds herself solving a dangerous kidnapping case.

Lifeboat (1944) is one of Hitchcock's most unusual films—albeit one of his least commercial. A group of men and women find themselves on a lifeboat after their ship is torpedoed by a German submarine. Also on board is a Nazi who pretends not to understand English. You can look at the film as an ensemble piece, but at the center is Constance Porter (Tallulah Bankhead), a reporter who first appears to be one of Hitchcock's cruelest, most self-absorbed characters. She reminds us of Charlotte Inwood, the manipulative and treacherous singer in *Stage Fright*. Constance cares more about capturing tragedy on her camera, typing up notes on the drama unfolding aboard the lifeboat, and making sure her fur coat and diamond bracelet are not lost at sea than she does about her fellow survivors. At one point, she declares that she is practically "immortal." Initially she and a blue-collar type named Kovac (played by John Hodiak) hate each other, but in the face of danger they bond, and she admits that she too is from a poor background. In her greatest line, she says, "Dying together is even more personal than

living together," an admission of her love for him and a recognition of his for her. "Tallulah was a real pro," Hitchcock said, "but I must say that she was tremendously extroverted. There were complaints that she was climbing in and out of the bright lights with nothing under her skirt."

All of Hitchcock's women fascinate, whether they were blonde or brunette, victim or threat, comedian or tragedian. And each one is a determined creation of the director's imagination. He cast them, then groomed them to fit his frame. He also took good care of them—just as he did his own wife and daughter. Women dominated his best work and it was thanks to them that his heroes became significant. In his private life, the same happened. His wife was the only one who noticed before *Psycho* was shipped to the theatres that Janet Leigh "swallowed" as she was lying dead on the bathroom floor. A quick cut to the showerhead allowed Hitchcock to remove the mistake. Hitchcock trusted his wife's intuition and never shipped a movie without her approval. And in return, he gave that same level of trust to the women he cast in his films.

As we have seen so far in the case of *The Birds* and *Marnie* particularly, when discussing women in Hitchcock's work, one cannot ignore the importance and influence of mothers in his films. Mothers are part of the problem—or part of the solution—either way, part of the tapestry of the story.

A relative of Alfred Hitchcock's said of the filmmaker's own mother, Emma Jane Whelan, that she was "a smartly dressed, sedate person, very quietly spoken with an aristocratic manner. She was very

ABOVE Barbara Harris, who played Madame Blanche in *Family Plot* (1976)

TOP RIGHT On the *Lifeboat* set with Tallulah Bankhead

BOTTOM RIGHT With Alma Reville working on the script of *Lifeboat*

meticulous when preparing a meal, at which she was very good. She would not venture out of her room unless perfectly dressed, and she quietly conducted her affairs in a dignified manner." Replace *she* with *he*, as in *Alfred*, and no one who knew him would blink. Mother and son were very similar.

Emma Jane Whelan was born in 1863 and came from an Irish Catholic background. She married William Hitchcock in 1887—he was twenty-four, her senior by one year. Although the portrayals of mothers in his films were not necessarily homages, Hitch loved Emma. As a child, he would come home from school and sit on her bed to answer questions about his day. After his father died (when Hitch was only fifteen years old), he grew even closer to her. In his adult life, Emma often accompanied him and Alma on their vacations. When the Hitchcocks moved to America in 1939, however, Emma chose to remain in England. Although it is probably a coincidence, Hitch's favorite film of all is *Shadow of a Doubt,* which he was making when his mother passed away. You can't help but watch that film with a sense that perhaps Hitchcock was paying tribute to her. The mother in the film, named Emma, is one of the nicest of all of his on-screen moms.

Another powerful portrayal of a mother is Doris Day's in the remake of *The Man Who Knew Too Much* (1956). Edna Best in the original version was also memorable, but not, curiously, as motherly as Doris Day was in the remake. (In fact, Edna Best is shown shamelessly flirting with a man other than her husband in the first version of that film.) "Although he had verbally communicated very little to me," Doris Day later recalled, "somehow, by some mystical process, I learned some important things about Hitchcock

moviemaking that were to serve me as well in the future. Certainly, a lesson about confidence."

As in the original *Man Who Knew Too Much,* a young couple befriends a man who is murdered shortly after they meet. He is a spy and before he dies, he reveals a secret to the husband (James Stewart in the remake). Jo McKenna (Doris Day) has given up her career as a successful singer to live a quiet life with her somewhat dull doctor husband. But she loves him, even if he thinks of them as an "old married couple." A heart-wrenching moment relies purely on Day's performance when her husband tells her that their son has been kidnapped. He gives her some sedative first, and her reaction is all the more powerful as she fights the drug meant to spare her. From that point forward, Jo travels the greater emotional journey. While her husband goes from one wild goose chase to the next, Jo winds up stopping the attempted assassination of a dignitary at a concert by screaming out loud during the crash of the cymbals, which was to be a signal to the killers to strike.

Besides mothers having a physical presence in many of his films, Hitchcock often has his female leads flirt by mixing maternal instinct with a seductive twist. Several of his female characters tease their male counterparts with a little bit of "Mama Knows Best."

LEFT Hitchcock drawing sketches for *Lifeboat* (1944)

ABOVE Doris Day and James Stewart in *The Man Who Knew Too Much* (1956)

Ingrid Bergman says to Cary Grant in *Notorious*, "Well, handsome, you better tell Mama what's going on." When Scottie, in *Vertigo,* asks Midge about her designing a brassiere, Midge says, "You know about those things. You're a big boy now." In *North by Northwest* Cary Grant says, "When I was a little boy, I wouldn't even let my mother undress me." Eva Marie Saint replies, "You're a big boy now." Other mother characters serve to set the plot in motion. If not for

his mother (played by Jessie Royce Landis) in *North by Northwest*, Roger Thornhill never would have been mistaken for the mysterious (and nonexistent) Kaplan, and there would have been no plot. As it plays out, Roger goes for drinks at the Plaza Hotel and needs to send a telegram to his mother. By hailing a page who is calling, "Telephone for Mr. George Kaplan," he is mistaken for Mr. George Kaplan by two villains. Later, Roger and his mom find themselves in the same elevator as the henchmen. She says, "You gentlemen aren't really trying to kill my son."

In *To Catch a Thief* Jessie Royce Landis plays Jessie Stevens, Grace Kelly's mother. She—naïvely—thinks of her daughter as virginal. "I'm sorry I ever sent her to that finishing school. I think they finished her there," she says, desperate for her daughter to marry a man like—perhaps—John Robie. Ironically,

Hitchcock ends *To Catch a Thief* on a comical remark from Grace Kelly. She has followed Robie to his home, which overlooks the Riviera, and after they've embraced, she says, not so innocently, "So this is where you live. Oh, Mother will love it up here!" And there's also Bruno Anthony's wacky mother (Marion Lorne) in *Strangers on a Train,* who leaves no doubt as to where her son inherited his madness.

Of course no mother dominates her child more than Norma Bates, whose son Norman says at one point in *Psycho,* "A boy's best friend is his mother." We only ever hear her voice, and later we find out it's really Norman impersonating her. Even so, Hitchcock gives Norma the last word, played out in Norman's head but in his mother's voice. Norman, arrested and in jail, looks up at the audience with a smirk and for a few frames, mother and son are one as Hitchcock dissolves to the permanent grin on the face of the decomposed corpse of Norma Bates.

The ambiguous mother-son theme is also present in *Notorious* represented by the intense relationship between Alex Sebastian (Claude Rains) and his mother (Leopoldine Konstantin). She is immediately suspicious of Alicia (Ingrid Bergman), and her son mistakes this for jealousy. Perhaps it is, but when he realizes that he has married an American agent, he runs to his mother's bedroom for help. She masterminds the demise of Alicia—by poison. "Let me arrange this one," she tells him, and she does her best, but ultimately fails. Madame Sebastian is more frightening than Alex. She is the villain in the movie, which, in the world of Hitchcock, is not always a negative trait. "Murder can be an art too," one of Hitchcock's characters says in *Rope.* "The power to kill can be as satisfying as the power to create." Some mothers might know.

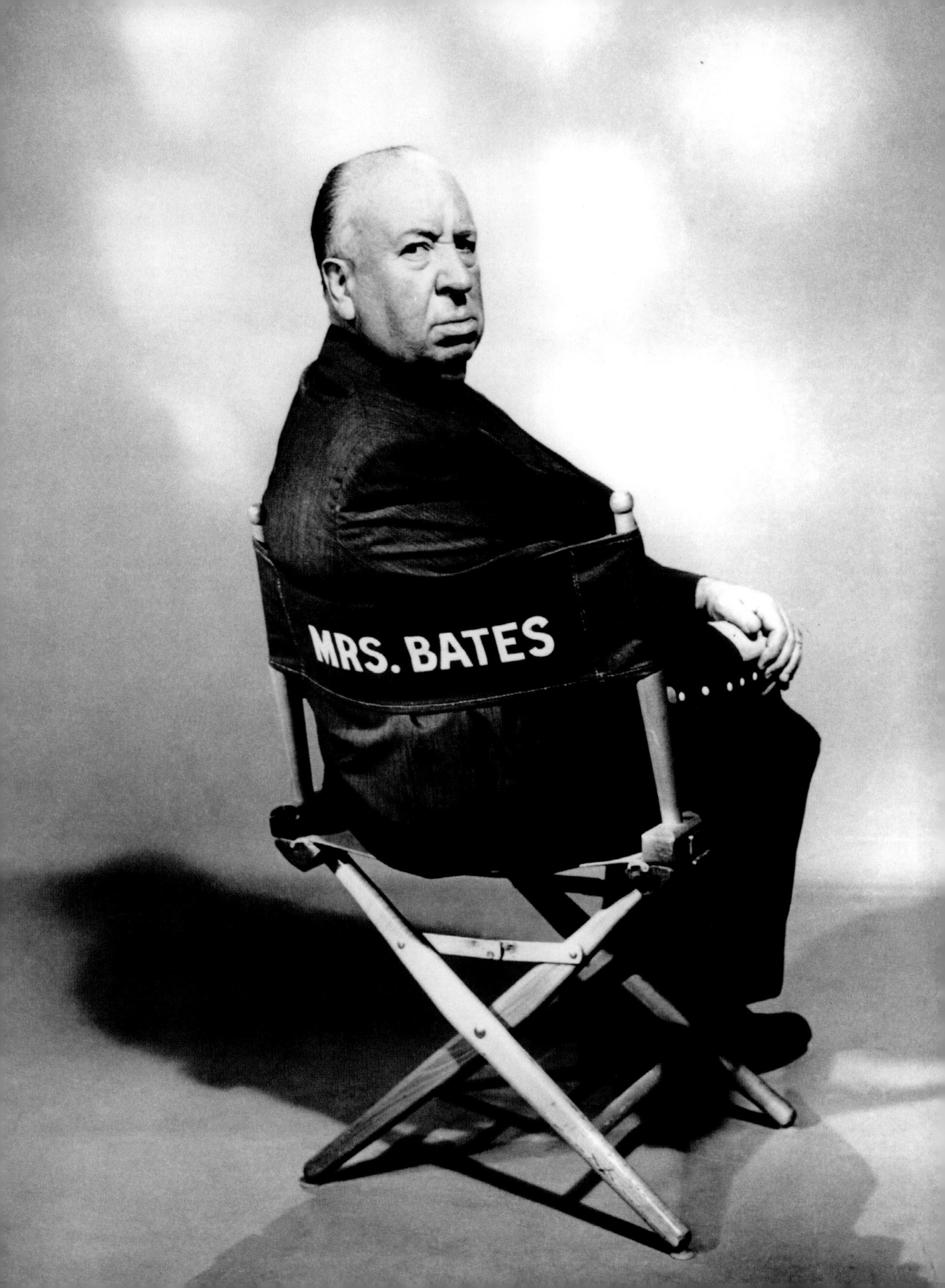
MRS. BATES

psychos and frenzies

CHAPTER III

The charming, disarming, deceiving villains in Hitchcock's films

RIGHT Anthony Perkins in *Psycho* (1960)

An Agatha Christie–type character in *Suspicion* (1941) says of the villains in her mystery novels, "I always think of my murderers as my heroes." This quote seems to parallel Hitchcock's own approach to the bad guys in his films. "I always make my villains charming and polite," the director said. "It's a mistake to think that if you put a villain on screen, he must sneer nastily, stroke his black mustache, or kick a dog in the stomach. Some of the most famous murderers in criminology—men for whom arsenic was so disgustingly gentle that they did women in with a blunt instrument—had to be charmers to get acquainted with the females they eventually murdered. The really frightening thing about villains is their surface likableness." Hitchcock was a master at making his killers almost as charm-

ing as his heroes. They all seem to possess a sense of humor, and though their view of the world is sinister, they keep smiles on their faces.

The spies or traitors are usually the "nicest" villains. There's Professor Jordan (Godfrey Tearle), who is missing part of a finger in *The 39 Steps* (1935), and Paul Lukas, the devious doctor of *The Lady Vanishes* (1938). In *Sabotage* (1936) Mr. Verloc (albeit creepy) still feels remorse when he inadvertently causes the death of his wife's brother. You wouldn't necessarily turn down an invitation to a meal from Sir Humphrey Pengallan (Charles Laughton) in *Jamaica Inn* (1939). You might let Dr. Murchison (Leo G. Carroll) from *Spellbound* (1945) psychoanalyze you—although he is revealed to be a deranged killer. You may trust Jacques Granville (Michel Piccoli),

the mastermind behind a spy ring called *Topaz* in the film of the same title (1969). Some of those characters are not introduced as villains, but rather as likable characters, such as the Robert Young role in *Secret Agent* (1936). A complete red herring, he initially seems to be used almost as comic relief until it turns out he is the traitor John Gielgud and Madeleine Carroll have been after all along. That twist is part of the suspense, which gives the audience an unanticipated shock when it learns that it has been sympathizing with the bad guy all along. Such is the character of Stephen Fisher played by Herbert Marshall in *Foreign Correspondent* (1940). We're introduced to him really through his daughter—who becomes the love interest of the hero played by Joel McCrea. Fisher has class; he is charming and sophisticated. Because he is blinded by love, McCrea's John-

ny Jones doesn't suspect Fisher—even when he warns Fisher about Mr. Krug (played by the frightening-looking Eduardo Ciannelli), a man Jones knows to be orchestrating dirty work. He tells Fisher that Krug is involved in the kidnapping of a diplomat who has a section of a major international treaty—on which the advent of war is hanging—committed to memory. When confronted with Jones's revelation, Fisher plays it cool, saying, "Leave it to me." But in the end, during a sensational climax in which a plane carrying Fisher, his daughter, and Jones, as well as other passengers comes under attack and crashes into the sea, the traitor sacrifices himself to allow others to live.

At the other end of the bad-guy spectrum, Mr. Krug in *Foreign Correspondent* represents the sort of henchman that Hitchcock would often pair up with his "champagne" villain. Krug, who is always

LEFT Godfrey Tearle, Helen Haye, Robert Donat, and Peggy Simpson in *The 39 Steps* (1935)
ABOVE With Paul Lukas on the set of *The Lady Vanishes* (1938)

seen wearing a turtleneck, is obviously a cold-blooded psychopath. During a fight, the turtleneck is pulled down to reveal a nasty scar across his throat, suggesting he may have had his head in a noose at some point. He's been to the gallows; he's committed a capital crime and somehow escaped death. *Foreign Correspondent* also showcases a third type of villain Hitchcock used, the fallible kind. Edmund Gwenn—a British player who Hitchcock had used in the past and would use again—plays a clumsy killer who, hired to kill Joel McCrea's Johnny Jones and make it look like an accident, winds up dead when he attempts to push the intended victim from the top of Winchester Cathedral.

Hitchcock would assemble a similar rogue's gallery in *Saboteur* (1942). There's Charles Tobin, played with great flair by Otto Kruger. Everybody thinks of

him as a true American, a gentleman who loves his baby granddaughter, but he is quite the opposite. All he wants, he confesses later, is power. He wants it as much as someone else would want comfort, a job, or a girl. "We all have different tastes," he says, but he is willing to back his desires with the necessary force to achieve them. Later, we meet a socialite played by Alma Kruger (no relation to Otto), who was a great character actress. She is matronly, nothing dark on the surface about her, but she, too, engages in traitorous activities. There's an accomplice, a man named Freeman played by Alan Baxter, a stage actor and wrestler, who brought a great ambiguity to his role. He has very mild and meek manners, but you can sense the madness and rage underneath. He only has a couple of scenes, but one specific moment offers shades of Norman Bates, revealing the dark-

ABOVE Hitchcock and Oscar Homolka on the set of *Sabotage* (1936)
RIGHT Norman Lloyd and Gregory Peck in *Spellbound* (1945)

ness beyond his surface appearance, as he comments on Tobin's love for his granddaughter. "Evidence of a good heart," he says. He himself has two boys, aged two and four. The eldest causes trouble, smashing his toys. "Sometimes, after it's all over, he seems almost sorry." As for his second boy, he wishes he had had a girl instead. "My wife and I often argue about a little idiosyncrasy I have. I don't want to have his hair cut short until he is much older." He reveals that as a child, he had long golden curls and that people used to admire him.

Saving the best for last, there's the henchman named Fry, played by Norman Lloyd, who would also appear as a patient in *Spellbound* and who later worked in various capacities on the Alfred Hitchcock television shows. Lloyd had been an actor for nine

years when he got a call from John Houseman, a partner in Orson Welles's Mercury Theatre. In 1941, Houseman was, like Hitchcock, under contract with David O. Selznick. Hitchcock was in New York for the opening of *Suspicion* and asked Houseman if he knew an actor who would be a good choice for the bad guy in *Saboteur*. Lloyd went to meet Hitchcock at the Saint Regis Hotel, where he was staying. Hitch was returning to Los Angeles, so Lloyd tested with another director. He selected a scene from a play called *Blind Alley* in which he played a mad killer— and got the part.

Lloyd had the perfect presence for the role and as a result was part of several great set pieces in the film. One takes place in a shipyard, where Robert Cummings's character Barry Kane tries to

stop him—unsuccessfully—from pressing a button that will detonate a bomb. Lloyd loved to move and during the confrontation, Hitchcock allowed him to fight with Robert Cummings almost like a gymnast. (He wore a special pair of shoes with crepe soles.) It was Hitchcock's idea to keep cutting back to Lloyd's finger nearly touching the button and then finally pressing it. This was followed by a chase at the Radio City Music Hall where Lloyd goes crazy and shoots at members of an audience watching a film—the audience at first thinks that the gunshots are coming from the screen.

The grand climax, and a scene that would highly influence the ending of *North by Northwest* (1959) on top of Mount Rushmore, involves Norman Lloyd in his showdown with Robert Cummings on top of the Statue of Liberty. Selecting the symbol of liberty for the closing of a film about traitors and the outbreak of war was, of course, intentional. The death of the villain is the most spectacular and suspenseful aspect of the film. Lloyd ends up barely hanging on,

and as Robert Cummings tries to pull him to safety, the fabric of his sleeve starts unraveling. In a series of brilliant cuts, we see Lloyd's hand slowly sliding out of the sleeve and then, finally, he falls backward. To this day the sequence is completely effective. To film it, a replica of the top of the Statue of Liberty was constructed on stage at Universal. For the fall, and with the collaboration of Robert Boyle and John Fulton, two visual geniuses on Hitchcock's crew, Lloyd was seated against black while the camera pulled away from him. Later, the black space was filled in with matte shots depicting the top of the statue and its background, giving the illusion that Lloyd was falling from a great height.

Hitchcock acknowledged he had made one big mistake in that scene; it should have been the hero, not the villain, in jeopardy. Later, in *North by Northwest*, he would have a chance to redo almost exactly the same scene, but this time with the villains on top, and Cary Grant and Eva Marie Saint below, fighting for their lives. (Grant is holding on to Eva Marie

ABOVE A replica of the Statue of Liberty's crown on the set of *Saboteur* (1942)

PAGE 105 Hitchcock during the filming of *North by Northwest* (1959)

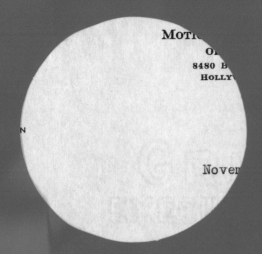

MOTIO
OI
8480 B
HOLLYV

N

Nover

HITCHCOCK
piece by piece

As you kn
hen restricted to
sions, is acceptabl
casual use of such ex
would like to suggest,
this script with the i
two which you feel are

You understand, o
will be based on the fi

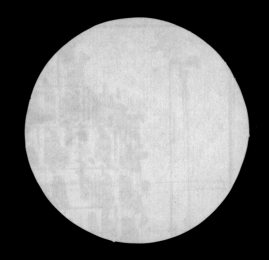

HITCHCOCK
piece by piece

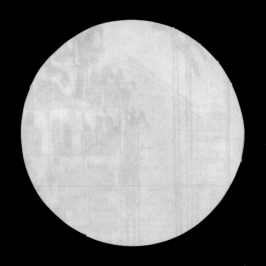

Saint, and he begs Leonard, played by Martin Landau, to help him. Instead, Landau steps on Grant's hand. Luckily, the police arrive and shoot him.) *Saboteur* remains an important film in Hitchcock's body of work not only in terms of the wrong man, the blonde, and the construction of his suspense sequences, but also in his design of his archetypal villains.

When Eve Kendall (Eva Marie Saint) says, "I met Philipp Vandamm at a party one night and saw only his charm," she could be describing exactly how Hitchcock is hoping audiences will respond to his villains in general. James Mason, who plays Vandamm, is indeed charming. He even runs his "business" like a party. Just as Tobin does in *Saboteur*, Mason's Vandamm remains composed and polite even when giv-

ing orders to kill. He has three henchmen—two with hardly any dialogue—and Martin Landau's Leonard, whom Vandamm describes as his right arm. When Landau first met Hitchcock for the role, he was shown storyboards rather than a script. Landau was not completely familiar with the master's work, but knew of such classics as *Strangers on a Train* (1951). When he finally read the role, he realized he had very few lines, and in an effort to bring more depth to Leonard, he asked Hitchcock if he could play him as a gay man. The director agreed, and indeed it seems that there is a special bond between Vandamm and Leonard. Perhaps Vandamm sees Leonard more as a son, but Leonard is clearly infatuated with his boss. This all comes to the surface when Leonard raises doubts about Eve Kendall. Vandamm's reaction is

classic. He laughs, tells Leonard that he is jealous of a woman, and that he is even flattered. He takes this as a compliment. Then Leonard reveals to Vandamm that Eve faked shooting Roger in cafeteria. She used blank cartridges. At that moment, Vandamm loses his temper for the first time. He is enraged and punches Leonard for unmasking Eve.

At one point, Roger Thornhill tells Vandamm, "The only performance that will satisfy you is when I play dead." And Vandamm replies, "Your very next performance. I assure you you'll be quite convincing." That line is the ultimate dream of the Hitchcockian villain—the perfect crime, the perfect death, getting away with murder. Plan it and get it done neatly.

Hitch's villains don't always take center stage in his films, but they motivate the action nonetheless. Examples of villains that set the plot in motion include the creepy Peter Lorre in the original *The Man Who Knew Too Much* (1934); the much more likable couple played by Bernard Miles and Brenda de Banzie in the remake of that same film (1956); Raymond Burr as Lars Thorwald in *Rear Window* (1954); and Gavin Elster in *Vertigo* (1958).

But then there are those villains who occupy the red-hot center of the film, such as Ray Milland in *Dial M for Murder* (1954). He is easily as fascinating as Vandamm, albeit of a different temperament (Milland's Tony Wendice is smarmy and insincere). His wife Margot, played by Grace Kelly, is guilt-ridden because she has a lover, Mark Halliday (Robert Cummings). She knows, as she says at the beginning of the film, that Tony has changed. She just doesn't suspect that the change is due to that the fact that he has finally come up with a way to kill her without getting his hands dirty.

Hitchcock always looked down on *Dial M for Murder* because it is essentially a filmed play. But in many ways and purely for entertainment value, it is far superior to *Lifeboat* (1944), although not as profound, and *Rope* (1948), two films that both take place in confined spaces, as does his subsequent film, *Rear Window* (1954). But unlike *Rear Window*, it's undeniable that the main focus of *Dial M for Murder* is the villain, just as the two psychopaths in *Rope* were the central characters of that story. The riveting aspect of Tony's role is that he has planned everything so well we root for him. Or at least our heart beats for him when things go wrong. Not that Hitchcock makes us feel sympathy for the villain, but he does make us part of the brilliant plan. Tony's biggest flaw is that he believes in the perfect murder. And, as he is reminded by Mark Halliday, a mystery

LEFT Cary Grant, Eva Marie Saint, James Mason, and Martin Landau in *North by Northwest* (1959)
ABOVE Peter Lorre in *The Man Who Knew Too Much* (1934)

writer, the perfect crime only exists on paper. Tony thinks he has found the one and only person to carry out the crime; he has selected a man named Lesgate (Anthony Dawson, who would play a key role in *Dr. No* [1962] several years later). Lesgate and Tony knew each other from school. Having lost contact years before, Tony explains he saw him by pure coincidence and began following him. It was clear in their youth that Lesgate was a thief and off to a bad start. Now, he is a criminal with many aliases who has not yet gotten caught, but he may if he doesn't do what Tony asks him to do. There you have the perfect contrast: the champagne villain with Milland and the somewhat hatchet-faced killer with Dawson. The stage is set for the perfect crime.

The attempted murder, as it turns out, is brilliantly choreographed by Hitchcock—and quite brutal for its time. One can easily see how gradually his murder scenes get more and more graphic, more and more disturbing. In this case, there's the suspense of Tony realizing his watch has stopped. He's playing bridge at his club for his alibi. The plan is for him to call his home at an appointed time, waking Margot, who will answer, making it easy for the killer to strangle her while she's on the phone. Hitchcock builds the suspense as Tony is outside an occupied phone booth, and Lesgate, tired of waiting, probably thinking Tony changed his mind, starts to walk away when finally the phone rings. Lesgate's attempt to strangle Margot is both seen *and* heard through the telephone. At that point, Ray Milland's performance takes on another tone; he almost feels sorry for his wife as he listens to her agony and struggle. But he quickly regains his cool when he realizes that something has gone wrong (his wife has actually stabbed Lesgate with a pair of scissors). She

is alive and the killer is dead. But the real villain is still there, and he now has to switch gears in order to pin murder on Margot. Tony makes it seem as if Margot killed Lesgate because he knew of her affair and was blackmailing her. In the end, the key to the mystery is literally the actual key to Tony and Margot's apartment—the key that the killer was supposed to have in his pocket when he entered the room to kill her. Tony always assumed he kept it in his pocket, whereas in fact the killer had replaced it where it was hidden before entering the apartment. Hence the French title of the film—*The Crime Was Almost Perfect*. The villain is caught, and after the initial shock of his defeat, he quickly turns to the bar and offers everyone a drink (except the inspector on duty).

Yes, you can love and admire *Notorious* (1946) for Ingrid Bergman and Cary Grant, but you can also love it for Claude Rains who, as Alex Sebastian, is a villain with an arc. One can easily imagine him as a child, short and awkward, not particularly attractive, a mama's boy. But he is blinded by his infatuation with Alicia Huberman (Ingrid Bergman), the daughter of a traitor. Rains's performance as an insecure husband who constantly (and rightly) feels threatened by Cary Grant, is brilliant, almost touching. He is like Philip Vandamm in *North by Northwest*, fooled by love and manipulated by a woman. But in the case of Alex, he is manipulated by two women: Alicia *and* his mother. When Alex finds out that he is married to an American agent, Hitchcock decides to film him from above, in a tight close-up, powerfully conveying his devastation and vulnerability. He becomes again the little kid who probably came to his mother's bedroom each time someone tormented him. Rains's

RIGHT Ingrid Bergman and Claude Rains in *Notorious* (1946)

performance continues to evolve as both mother and son conspire to poison Alicia. He becomes cocky with his newly found control, until Cary Grant realizes what's happening and rescues Alicia. *Notorious* ends with Rains's feared accomplice, Eric Mathis (played by Ivan Triesault), saying, "Alex, will you come in, please. I wish to talk to you." We know that for both mother and son, the end is near. Hitchcock gives the last word to Mathis who, in essence, is an even greater villain than Alex and his mother.

As we've established earlier, it's almost impossible to think of Hitchcock without thinking of *Psycho* (1960) and Norman Bates. In fact, it's probably impossible to think of cinema without evoking immediately *Psycho,* its villain, and the indelible performance by Anthony Perkins as the disturbed young man. It's a role that would, for better or for worse, haunt the actor for the rest of his career. His unforgettable performance made it a challenge to think of him as anyone but Norman Bates. The character in the film is much more complex than the unattractive, reclusive character in Robert Bloch's original novel. But the name *Norman,* which originated in the book, is, as explained by Bloch himself, the combination of *nor* and *man,* since Norman is neither man nor woman. Bloch also said that he may have been influenced by the name of a well-known female impersonator named Karyl Norman. *Bates* is a pun on the word *baits* and how Norman baits his victims.

Robert Bloch was living in northern Wisconsin when he wrote *Psycho.* The story was loosely based on the notorious serial killer Ed Gein, who lived in Plainfield, Wisconsin, thirty-nine miles from Bloch's own house. Gein was a fifty-one-year-old handyman

when he was arrested in 1957 on suspicion of having murdered a middle-aged woman. The police conducted a search of his house and discovered a ghastly crime scene. It turned out Gein was a serial killer who had kept body parts. Bloch was familiar with the case when he started writing his book—but it was only later that he discovered how closely Norman Bates resembled Gein. The notion of Norman's split personality can be found in two of Bloch's early short stories: "Lucy Comes to Stay," in which a woman tells of the crimes committed by her best friend Lucy—until we discover that there is no Lucy; and "The Real Bad Friend," which is the story of a seemingly normal man who takes on the personality of an imaginary friend in order to murder his wife. But when Bloch, who was never approached to write the script, saw *Psycho* for the first time, he told Hitchcock that it was going to be either his best or worst film!

As seen through the character of Norman Bates, *Psycho* is the ultimate thriller, but also a tragedy. Bates is not responsible for his actions, and what makes the audience have some sympathy for him is the way Hitchcock introduces the character. He is gawky, awkward, clearly dominated by his (off-screen) mother, and sexually repressed. Looking back at the film, it's easy to recognize the signs of his madness. But when the film first came out, Hitchcock begged his audience not to reveal the film's ending. "It's the only one we've got," he said. He approached his ultimate villain as a victim, almost in the same way he had depicted his wrong men.

Anthony Perkins defined what it meant to play a real psychopath, but he was never able to shake that role or, arguably, to play any other type of character in the same compelling way. "Tony and I were already

friends when we worked on *Psycho*," Janet Leigh said. "We really had a great time on the set. He was really easy to deal with and at the same time, he was extremely intense, well-prepared, and professional." Tony Perkins is truly unforgettable in that role—the range of his performance in that film shows the depth through which Hitchcock understood the character and nature of someone like Norman Bates.

One could easily see Norman Bates as the culmination of Hitchcock's previous psychos. In *Shadow of a Doubt* (1943), Uncle Charlie, a remorseless killer of rich widows, has no respect for society and holds a dark view of the world. Hitchcock doesn't try to explain his motivation beyond one scene at the beginning. His sister, played by Patricia Collinge, explains how Charlie grew up a quiet boy who

was always reading. Then his father bought him a bicycle, and he went off on an icy road and skidded into a streetcar. He fractured his skull and almost died. "[W]hen he was getting well, there was no holding him. It was just as though all the rest was, well, too much for him and he had to get into mischief to blow off steam. He didn't do much reading after all that, let me tell you." Indeed, he became a killer instead! Hitchcock uses images of smoke and clouds to foreshadow his menace. When Uncle Charlie arrives in Santa Rosa, there's dark smoke coming out of the train, clouding up the perfectly clear sky. Later, when Charlie is reading the paper, looking for stories that may incriminate him, smoke from his cigar rises from behind the pages. We know that his rage is building, and we also know there's a story about one of his crimes in the paper.

ABOVE Joseph Cotten in *Shadow of a Doubt* (1943)

Making Uncle Charlie even more frightening is the way Joseph Cotten's performance switches effortlessly back and forth between being charming one minute and terrifying the next. His niece Charlie is his double—his good twin—the part of him that died in his childhood accident. And when he tries to kill her aboard a moving train at the end of the film, it's literally a fight between good and evil. Uncle Charlie slips and is run over by an oncoming train, defeated, but not completely vanquished. Young Charlie has looked into the dark side; she now knows that it exists and, as her uncle warned her at the beginning of the film, "it's not good to find out too much."

Joseph Cotten, the man, couldn't have been further from the twisted personality he portrayed in the film. "Joseph Cotten was a very close friend of my parents. And I had an enormous crush on him!" Pat Hitchcock said. "I recall that the making of that film was just very happy. There was a real family atmosphere on the set."

Uncle Charlie's philosophy of life is sprinkled throughout the film. He loves details, "all the little details." He admires people who face facts. He loves the past, hates the present. "The whole world is a joke to me," he says. He hates the world so much that he doesn't care what happens in it. He hates rich widows, doesn't think they're human beings, and compares them to animals. "What happens to animals when they get too fat and too old?" We know that Uncle Charlie has formed an answer to that question for himself. His arrogant belief that he can take lives, that he has power over those he feels are "animals" and therefore inferior to him, makes Uncle Charlie a distant cousin to the two psychopaths from Hitchcock's *Rope*.

Rope (1948) started with a British play called *Rope's End* by Patrick Hamilton and a story treatment by Hume Cronyn. The script for the film was written by Arthur Laurents, who had written *The Snake Pit* (1948). Although he was uncredited on the film, that great work prepared him for his collaboration with Hitchcock. What intrigued Laurents was that *Rope* was really about two homosexuals who were lovers, yet the word was never mentioned, not by Hitchcock, and not by the studio. It was in fact referred to as "It." The story was loosely based on a true story (the American Leopold-Loeb case in which two young men murdered a boy as an intellectual challenge to commit the perfect crime). Laurents adapted the British play to an American setting. John Dall and Farley Granger played the two lead characters, Brandon and Philip.

It is important to note how daring it was to have two killers in the leading roles. Brandon is the cool, composed type, although he does stutter when "he gets excited." (Norman Bates stutters as well, when he gets nervous.) Philip is the paranoid type. The film begins with the murder of one of their college friends, David. They strangle him, put him in a chest in the middle of their apartment, and proceed to prepare for the party they are hosting later that same day. The invited guests include the victim's family, his girlfriend, and their teacher, Rupert Cadell (James Stewart). The teacher has apparently influenced the two young men with his philosophical talk about the "Superman." At the party, Cadell is grumpy, misogynistic to a point, but slowly realizes what's going on. When he makes the grim discovery that his pupils have put his theories into practice, he shoots a gun outside the window, alerting neighbors to call the police. As in *The Trouble with Harry*, there's great dark humor in the film. But there's also something extremely disturbing about *Rope*. Like Uncle Charlie, Brandon has a defining take on the world. He feels that being weak is a flaw because it's being ordinary. He thinks that good and evil, right and wrong, were invented for the ordinary, average man, the inferior man, "because he needs them." Philip, it appears, has gone along with the plan of killing their college friend because of the power that Brandon has over him. "You frighten me," he tells him. "You always have. From that very first day in prep school. Part of your charms, I suppose." But for Brandon, David is the perfect victim for the perfect crime; he is not one of those good Americans who died young on the battlefield. He merely occupies space. Hence his theory that murder can be an art, that the power to kill can be as satisfying as the power to create. Brandon and Philip killed for the sake of danger and for the sake of killing. Brandon enjoys the novelty in this; nobody kills just for the experience—"except for us!" While murder is a crime for most, it is their right.

With that in mind and despite its humor, *Rope* is one of Hitchcock's darkest films, with two of his most disturbing villains at center stage.

Brandon, particularly with his crazy theories, comes close to Bruno Anthony (Robert Walker), the psychopathic killer that Guy Haines (Farley Granger) encounters in *Strangers on a Train* (1951). Like Brandon, he also is obsessed with the perfect crime. "Want to hear one of my ideas about the perfect murder?" he asks. "You want to hear the busted light socket in the bathroom or the carbon monoxide in the garage?" To him, murder is a game, and he believes he

has found in Guy the perfect partner. Since Guy is a famous tennis champion, his private life is public knowledge, so Bruno is aware that Guy is trying to get a divorce so he can marry a senator's daughter. Bruno hates his own father and decides they should swap murders—his father for Guy's wife. Bruno carries out his side of the bargain and then expects Guy to do the same. Like Brandon in *Rope*, Bruno is amusing, funny, charming, and has great taste in clothes. Casting Robert Walker in the role was really going against what audiences expected from him. His son, Robert Walker, Jr., was eight years old at the time the film was being made and simply couldn't believe that his father was playing a bad guy. Yet, when he saw the final film, he recalls loving his father's performance, "not because it was Dad in the role, but because he was just such a great, charming bad guy!"

In addition to being a killer, Walker's character becomes a stalker. Because Guy won't fulfill his side of the bargain, Bruno starts following Guy everywhere. One of the most memorable scenes has Walker showing up uninvited at a party. He starts talking murder with two elderly women, and he asks one of them if he can "borrow" her neck in order to show how to strangle someone. But even with his most fearless villains, Hitchcock always inserts a hint of humanity in them. In that same scene, for instance, Pat Hitchcock, who plays Barbara Morton, the younger sister of the woman Guy wants to marry, shows up just as Bruno is pretending to strangle the elderly lady. Barbara is wearing the same glasses Guy's wife wore when Bruno murdered her. Suddenly, Bruno is transported back to the crime and faints. Just like Brandon's stuttering in *Rope*, Bruno's fainting shows that he is not invincible. Although those villains want

RIGHT On the set of *Rope* (1948)

to play God by taking an innocent victim's life, they are human, whether they like to think of themselves that way or not. Or better yet, as Guy says at the end of *Strangers on a Train* when someone asks him who Bruno was, he simply replies "a very clever fella."

Another "clever fella" is Richard Todd in *Stage Fright* (1950). He plays a man so infatuated with a manipulative woman (Marlene Dietrich) that he'd kill for her, which is what she wants and what he does. But he convinces Jane Wyman (and the audience) of his innocence. At the climax, Jane Wyman has just helped him escape from the police when she realizes that she was blinded by love, and instead of helping an innocent man, she is in the company of a dangerous killer. At that point, Todd's perform-

ance is frightening because his demeanor completely changes. The performance foreshadows that of Anthony Perkins as Norman Bates. Todd's insanity is as convincing as his declaration of innocence is at the beginning of the film. In his final speech he tells Jane Wyman that if he killed her, "that would be a clear case of insanity, wouldn't it?" Interestingly, this echoes Ingrid Bergman's confrontation with Leo G. Carroll in *Spellbound* when she finally realizes that he is the killer who framed Gregory Peck. He explains, "You forget in your imbecilic devotion to your patient that the punishment for two murders is the same as for one." Bergman then tries to convince him that a man with his intelligence does not commit a *stupid* murder. She eventually exits the room, and we follow her from the killer's point of view, looking

down the barrel of the gun he is holding. Eventually he turns the weapon on himself (with the barrel now pointing at us, the audience) and pulls the trigger! It's a sensational shot that for a few seconds puts us in the uncomfortable position of the criminal.

Of all Hitchcock's villains, Bob Rusk, as played by Barry Foster in *Frenzy* (1972), is the nastiest. The depiction of his crimes is extremely graphic, and Foster's interpretation of the role is inspired, but also unpleasant. We know the second he walks into a room that something awful is going to happen. At the time of *Frenzy*, Foster had had some success on stage and had done some interesting work on television. One evening, while doing a play by David Mercer called *After Haggerty* with Billie Whitelaw (who has a supporting role in *Frenzy*), Foster found out that

Hitchcock was in the audience. The next morning he received a call from his agent saying that a meeting had been set with the director at the MGM building, 100 Piccadilly. "I'm doing a film about a murderer," Hitchcock apparently said to Barry Foster. "I'd like you to read the script and tell me if you'd like to play the role." Along with the script, Hitchcock gave Foster a couple of books on serial killers, including one about Neville George Clevely Heath, who masqueraded as a squadron leader and lured one of his female victims to the Coburg Hotel, a location featured in *Frenzy*. Foster took the role, convinced that Hitchcock had decided on him because he had seen him on stage. Then, half way into shooting, he discovered through Hitch's personal assistant Peggy Robertson that he had in fact been chosen because of a part he had played in a cult film (often referred to as Hitchcock-

LEFT Robert Walker and Norma Varden in *Strangers on a Train* (1951)
ABOVE Marlene Dietrich and Richard Todd in *Stage Fright* (1950)

ian) called *Twisted Nerve* (1968), also starring Billie Whitelaw, with a score by Bernard Herrmann (who had written music for several Hitchcock films).

The most disturbing sequence in the film is the murder of Barbara Leigh-Hunt. Foster said it was precisely storyboarded, "which was incredibly helpful to us. And then, Barbara and I sort of gritted our teeth and went on with it!" As unpleasant as the scene may be for the audience, it wasn't necessarily the same filming it. Foster described the experience as a "mechanical" procedure at times, particularly when he had to lie down on a platform and pretend that he was raping his victim. But when performing directly with Barbara Leigh-Hunt, the actor acknowledged that the experience was "extremely distressing" for both of them. They relied on each other and consoled each other at the end of the day (the scene apparently took three days to shoot). "It leaves a mark on you," Foster acknowledged. "You have to go to the borders of human experience sometimes. It was the camaraderie between Barbara and me that got us through it."

It was reported by both Foster and screenwriter Anthony Shaffer that at the end of the scene, Hitchcock had shot a close-up of blood and saliva coming out of the victim's mouth. When he saw the scene, Shaffer told Hitchcock, "You have very successfully trod a tightrope between the sinister and the deeply worrying and unpleasant, but so far, have stayed clear of the completely unacceptable. [With that close-up], you have crossed that line and you are going to lose your audience if you keep that shot in. 'Nonsense, dear boy,' was the response." Yet the shot never made it to the final cut—instead, you may notice a freeze frame on the victim's face with her tongue sticking out. Sticking out, indeed—either at the screenwriter or at us, the audience, as a warning that things could have been a lot worse!

Two villains who are rarely acknowledged in the Hitchcock parade of bad guys are John Vernon, as the heartless revolutionary Rico Parra, and Michel Piccoli, as the traitorous Jacques Granville, in *Topaz* (1969). The film was not one of Hitchcock's most successful, but it remains a fascinating title with some very suspenseful scenes. The story concerns the Cuban missile crisis, a Russian defector, and a spy ring called *Topaz*. The film starred John Forsythe (in his second role for Hitchcock after *The Trouble with Harry*) as one of the good guys, along with Frederick Stafford.

"Hitchcock was determined to make a good film out of the novel [by Leon Uris]," Forsythe said. "But it's my opinion that he only succeeded in making what I thought was a brilliantly photographed, beautifully done picture. . . . The story elements were not as good as they should have been." When Hitchcock talked about *Topaz* to Forsythe, he said it was going to be very gutsy, full of adventure and romance. The one moment that everyone cites occurs when the villain Rico Parra kills Karin Dor's character, Juanita de Cordoba. When Rico, who is in love with her, discovers she has betrayed him with an American, he shoots her. She is wearing a beautiful purple gown. From a high angle, we see her fall to the ground. Her gown spreads around her like a fading flower, but also like a pool of purple blood. "He was a genius in getting individual shots," Forsythe said. "He was a most unusual man and the possessor of an incredible imagination and ability to transpose thought into action."

LEFT With Karin Dor and John Vernon on the set of *Topaz* (1969)

The ending of the film became an enormous challenge, similar to Hitch's situation when he was trying to find an effective ending for *Suspicion*. For *Topaz*, he had three separate endings. The first was a duel between Michel Piccoli and Frederick Stafford—a real duel, set in a deserted stadium (Piccoli's character, Granville, was having an affair with the hero's wife). The idea was as old-fashioned as the manner in which the two characters wanted to resolve their differences. "I thought it was something outside the film," Forsythe said, "and it was done to bring some excitement to the end of the picture." But it didn't work at all. Another ending was shot in which the hero and Granville cross paths at the airport, as Granville is leaving for Russia and André Devereaux (Stafford) and his wife are returning to America. Still dissatisfied with the outcome, a final ending was fashioned using a shot of a character entering Gran-

ville's place (just the end of the shot, so the audience would think it was Granville, but it was in fact a shot of another actor—Philippe Noiret), followed by a freeze-frame and a single gunshot off-screen, leading us to believe the bad guy had killed himself. Still, *Topaz* always felt like it didn't end properly. "The beginning and ending of a film are essential," Forsythe said. And in the case of *Topaz*, there simply wasn't a proper resolution, perhaps because neither the villains nor the hero and his ladies were compelling enough.

It wouldn't be accurate to think that Hitchcock only had male villains. Aside from mothers we've already mentioned, who could forget the evil Mrs. Danvers from his first American film, *Rebecca* (1940)? Jumping right out of the imagination of author Daphne du Maurier, Mrs. Danvers (played to perfection by Judith Anderson) is pure evil and immediately threatening

HITCHCOCK
piece by piece

HITCHCOCK
piece by piece

to the "second" Mrs. de Winter (Joan Fontaine). In fact, she is more evil and more manipulative than Jack Favell (George Sanders), Rebecca's "favorite cousin" and lover, who later attempts to blackmail Maxim. Danvers is obsessed with the memory of Rebecca—and was obviously infatuated with her. At one point, she shows Max's new wife a nightgown she had personally made for Rebecca and says, "Look, you can see my hand through it." No deeper explanation is needed here. Mrs. Danvers is fascinating in that she is at times purely cold with a business-like attitude (as in a scene where she asks that the new wife pick out the sauce for each item on a menu she has prepared), and at times, she seems completely mad (as in the scene where she tries to convince the heroine to commit suicide). In the novel, Danvers doesn't perish after setting Manderley on fire, but it was thought to be the most satisfying conclusion for the film.

Of course, the ultimate villain in the film is the woman we never meet: Rebecca herself, a woman who manipulated Max de Winter into marrying her, cheated on him through their marriage, and eventually continued to torment him beyond her own death. Not unlike Mrs. Bates in *Psycho*, Rebecca is the unseen, unmet villain, yet we see the destructive path that she left behind.

However awful, Rebecca must have had something, some bewitching quality that made Max de Winter fall in love with her in the first place. Whatever that was, Maddelena Anna Paradine (Alida Vali) must have possessed it, too. In *The Paradine Case* (1947), she is accused of murdering her husband, and Gregory Peck, who plays Anthony Keane, the attorney hired to defend her, falls in love with her. As if under a spell, he believes in her innocence. His infatuation with his client nearly costs him his marriage and his reputation—particularly when Mrs. Paradine ends up

admitting her guilt. At one point in the film, he goes to visit the mansion where she lived with her husband. As he enters her bedroom, the audience immediately feels the woman's strong presence, just as in *Rebecca* when Mrs. Danvers gives a tour of her former mistress's quarters, or when Vera Miles feels the bed where Mrs. Bates's body had been lying until Norman moved her corpse to the fruit cellar. The strength of evil emanating from these women seems at its most potent in their absence.

An all-time favorite Hitchcock villain is Charlotte Inwood (Marlene Dietrich) in *Stage Fright* (1950). She plays an actress/singer whose husband has been murdered. Hitchcock makes us believe that she killed him. Although it turns out Charlotte is innocent of murder, she did set up her lover to get rid of her husband. Charlotte Inwood is plain wicked and Dietrich plays her to perfection. In one scene, she performs a song by Cole Porter, "The Laziest Gal in Town." She is anything but lazy as she diligently uses all the men around her to get exactly what she wants.

Dietrich always reflected with great fondness on her time in *Stage Fright*. She became a good friend of the Hitchcocks and was particularly kind to the director's daughter, Pat—she explained to her movie lighting and how important it was to be lit a certain way. Filmmaker Peter Bogdanovich remembered once seeing Dietrich performing "The Laziest Gal in Town" at a concert and introducing the song by mentioning her work on *Stage Fright* for Hitchcock—putting a strong accent on the second syllable of his name. Wicked indeed.

For his last film, *Family Plot* (1976), Hitchcock combined many aspects of his previous villains. There's Arthur Adamson (William Devane), a psychopath with great charm and class—the killer of

LEFT With Alida Valli, on the set of *The Paradine Case* (1947)

ABOVE Marlene Dietrich, Hector MacGregor, and Hitchcock on the set of *Stage Fright* (1950)

his adoptive parents, a man who kidnaps people and asks for diamonds as ransom. He has two partners in crime—one played by Ed Lauter, who does his dirty work, and the other by Karen Black, who wears a blonde wig when she is collecting ransoms.

William Devane was perfect casting for Adamson. He was Hitch's first choice, but was apparently not available. So Roy Thinnes was hired. After a few days of filming, Hitchcock learned that Devane had become free. Although a great actor, Thinnes was

replaced and certain scenes were reshot, but not all. It appears that some of the long shots when the villains kidnap a priest in San Francisco may still feature Roy Thinnes, not Devane.

The way Hitchcock described Adamson to Devane was to tell him, "William Powell," the actor in the famous *Thin Man* comedy-thriller film series, and Adamson does have the twinkle that Powell had in those classic films, which confirms how much Hitchcock wanted audiences to like his villains. As for Karen Black, the actress initially wanted the role of the clairvoyant, Madame Blanche. But Hitchcock wanted Black for the villain and cast Barbara Harris

for the other role. The performances (and the dark humor) in *Family Plot* are in fact the most memorable aspects of the film. Good guys, bad guys, blondes, brunettes, psychos, and average men thrown in unusual circumstances all showed up for Hitchcock's goodbye to his audience. In a way, he was reminding us and inviting us to go back and check out all the other amazing characters that had led up to this final curtain call. And so we did and still do.

Of all Hitchcock's villains, one group stands alone: the birds from *The Birds* (1963). On the surface the film presents itself almost as a monster movie in which birds turn on the town of Bodega Bay. It followed the enormous success of *Psycho,* and in a way, Hitchcock had to top himself. In both cases, the villains truly are the stars of the stories. *The Birds* is a project that Hitch mentioned to his production designer Robert Boyle when he asked him to read the story by Daphne du Maurier. He was interested in getting Boyle's opinion on how the birds could be represented on screen— if he didn't have his villains, he didn't have a film. Although the story hardly has anything to do with the final plot of the film, Boyle was very enthusiastic about the potential and the challenge the film presented. After reading the story, he immediately went to his drafting table. The first image that came to him was the famous painting by Edvard Munch entitled "The Scream." That image inspired the horror and chaos the birds would create. Boyle then began investigating how the birds could be physically put into scenes. He solved this puzzle by using a process created by a man named Ub Iworks. Harold Michaelson was the main illustrator on the film and because of the technical aspect of the film, many sketches, storyboards, and

ABOVE William Devane and Karen Black in *Family Plot* (1976)

drawings were required to help visualize the elements involved in each scene. The end result would feature the combined efforts of Robert Boyle and his team, legendary matte artist Albert Whitlock, real birds provided by trainer Ray Berwick (since the idea of using mechanical birds was quickly abandoned), and innovative sound design with Bernard Herrmann collaborating with Remi Gassman and Oskar Sala, replacing what would have been a musical score.

The attacks were impressive. Each of them had a unique set-up. It starts with a single seagull plunging in on Melanie Daniels (Tippi Hedren), and from that point on the attacks become more and more threatening. One great and memorable scene involves Tippi Hedren smoking a cigarette outside in the school's playground. Several birds land behind her on the jungle gym, and as she continues to smoke, she eventually looks up. Her gaze follows a bird in the sky. As she watches it land behind her, she realizes that what appears to be hundreds of birds have gathered on the jungle gym, ready to go into full attack on the

children after school is over. The film is full of such surprises. We witness the violence the birds wrought on the corpse of a farmer whose eyes have been gouged. We see the birds in action as they cause a gas station to explode. But the most frightening scene involves Melanie alone as she enters a room that has been completely devastated by the birds; she is pushed against the door and the birds savagely attack her. That scene alone is as powerful as Janet Leigh's murder in *Psycho*.

The birds of *The Birds* do remain Hitchcock's most unpredictable villains. From a technical stand-point, the film may have been experimental. But from a story standpoint, Hitchcock stayed true to his usual portrayal of the antagonist in his films. And as in *Psycho*, Hitchcock gives the last word to his villains. In *The Birds*, as we watch our heroes drive away from Bodega Bay, Hitchcock concludes the film on the birds themselves, calm for now, but as all villains, ready to spring out and kill again—but purely for our entertainment.

the hitchcock touch

CHAPTER IV

*Signature innovations
of a master's craft*

Visually, Hitchcock approached murder with style. "Crime must be stylish," Hitchcock used to say. "It must have imagination and originality. I believe, furthermore, that logic is dull. I approach crime with fantasy."

But really, everything about a Hitchcock movie had something to do with style. His approach was unique. This led his audiences to expect certain things when they went to a Hitchcock film. His cameo appearances, for one thing—and then, of course, everything else. When Hitchcock began his career during the silent era, film was still experimental. His talent and vision evolved with the industry itself. Hitchcock broke ground on so many fronts, and all the while his visual language became more and more refined. As he added to his body of work, certain Hitchcockian themes emerged. Some, as we've seen, related to his stories, characters, and actors; others related to food (a constant in both the depiction of romance and murder). In the late summer of 1956, a fascinating lexicon written by Philippe Demonsablon appeared in the French film magazine *Les Cahiers du Cinéma* listing objects, themes, and other Hitchcockian trademarks that recurred in the master's work. It showed at that time that Hitchcock had created an oeuvre worthy of study and discussion. And while we've seen the thematic links to Hitchcock's films, specific objects that drive suspense, enhance the plot, or reveal the emotional make-up of particular characters also reappear. Equally significant, certain kinds of music and particular sounds have come to be identified with a Hitchcock film. But above all these elements, however, the director's original camerawork reigns.

Hitchcock's philosophy about filmmaking made the director central to every aspect of a given film.

"Directing a film, to me," he said, "is not just lining up shots and going home." Hitchcock searched for locations and worked closely with the screenwriters and his other collaborators. He also surrounded himself with the same crew over most of his career. Nothing unusual there—it's the way most successful directors are able to maintain a through-line not only over the course of one film, but over a body of work. There is also a shorthand dialogue that develops among colleagues after a while. Everyone knows what's expected, what's the routine, and how best to satisfy the man at the helm of the movie—in this case, Alfred Hitchcock.

Robert Boyle, who met Hitchcock on *Saboteur* (1942) and would go on to work in the art department or as production designer on four other Hitchcock films, immediately hit it off with the director. "Hitchcock was such a wonderful communicator. He said what he wanted and he drew rough sketches. And then, he'd just scribble over it. He would say [when referring to the fire at the factory in *Saboteur*], I want smoke to come in like that. Of all the directors I had worked with up to that point, this was the first time someone not only told me what they wanted but showed it to me as well. Hitchcock also liked to shoot on a stage versus going on location. He'd do his big establishing shots on location and then come into a set, where he had control over the light and noise." Hitchcock loved talking about process, according to Boyle. "He was very generous with discussing how he worked," Boyle recalled. "He loved to talk about it."

Excellence was the norm on any of his films because Hitchcock brought nothing less. He was so prepared by the time he got on the set that he never looked

LEFT Hitchcock drawing sketches for *Rebecca* (1940)

Innocent, *The Lady Vanishes, Shadow of a Doubt, Rope, Strangers on a Train, Dial M for Murder, Vertigo, Frenzy*), stabbing (think, for example, of *Blackmail, Murder!, The 39 Steps, Sabotage, Dial M for Murder,* the remake of *The Man Who Knew Too Much, North by Northwest, Psycho, Torn Curtain*), gunshot (watch for guns in *The Man Who Knew Too Much, The 39 Steps, Foreign Correspondent, Spellbound, To Catch a Thief, Topaz*), poison (order it à la carte in *Suspicion, Notorious, Under Capricorn, The Paradine Case, Psycho*) or other methods (see *Secret Agent, Sabotage, Rebecca, Lifeboat, Stage Fright, I Confess, Rear Window, The Trouble with Harry, Marnie*). François Truffaut sums up Hitchcock's cinematic murders this way: "In America, you respect him because he shoots scenes of love as if there were scenes of murder. In France, we respect him because he shoots scenes of murder like scenes of love."

Hitchcock also developed collaborative friendships with writers and actors. Hume Cronyn worked in both capacities with Hitch on several projects, and they remained close friends until Hitch died. They first met on *Shadow of a Doubt* (1943) in which Cronyn played the next-door neighbor, the one whose mother is always ill. Cronyn had done a screen test at Paramount that Hitchcock saw almost by chance. Summoned to meet with producer Jack Skirball in California, Cronyn was told he was too young for the part, but he still met with Hitch.

through the camera. He trusted his director of photography (like Robert Burks, who made twelve films with Hitchcock) as much as he trusted the actors he had hired. He did Pure Cinema—films that, in essence, were defining a language unique to a director. It's amazing when it comes to Hitchcock how often people will point out specific shots that left an impression on them. The shower sequence in *Psycho* (1960), for instance, is always cited as defining not only terror, but also shock in relation to the story (the female lead being killed early on in the narrative arc). It's also referred to again and again because of the way it was made—a series of shots, cut together very scientifically to obtain this groundbreaking effect that gave the illusion that the actress was actually being stabbed, so that you saw more than there was on the screen. We described earlier the aftermath of the murder in *Psycho*; it is perhaps just as devastating as the killing itself. Killing, dying, and mortal threats were an art form for Hitchcock, whether it was by strangulation (as, for instance, in *Young and*

ABOVE With James Stewart on the set of *The Man Who Knew Too Much* (1956)

RIGHT On the set of *Psycho* (1960)

"He had his hands tucked under his armpits with his thumbs straight up," Cronyn recalled. He asked the actor if he had ever been to Northern California, where the film was to be shot. Cronyn had never been there, but was quickly told that it was a wonderful wine country, and that after filming they'd go out into the vineyards "and we'll seize the grapes and we will squeeze the juice down our throats!" It looked like he had the part—and when Cronyn mentioned that he might look too young, Hitch simply said that they would age him. "I not only got to be in two of his films, *Shadow of a Doubt* and *Lifeboat*, but to also write the treatments for *Rope* and *Under Capricorn*," Cronyn said.

Cronyn credits Hitchcock for a valuable acting lesson. During one scene in *Shadow of a Doubt*, Cronyn kept taking a step in. Hitchcock had him do the scene over again, asking him not to move. Cronyn tried to explain that he felt it was necessary for his character to make a step during that moment. But he did as directed. Later, when Hitchcock showed him the dailies, Cronyn could see that Hitchcock had so clearly orchestrated the scene that his stepping in was meaningless. "That's something I never forgot," Cronyn said.

It was Hume Cronyn's observation that Hitchcock loved to be "enormously challenged and was stimulated by having a problem in the making of a film." Especially when people told him something would be impossible to realize. "For instance, when he did *The Birds* [1963] [Hume Cronyn's wife Jessica Tandy played Rod Taylor's mother], everyone was asking him, how are you going to collect that many birds?

ABOVE Hitchcock's cameo appearance in *Lifeboat* (1944)

How are you going to train them? It will be madness!! And you'll never keep on schedule." This attitude was also true of *Lifeboat*. Everyone wondered how Hitchcock would deal with a film that takes place exclusively inside a lifeboat. The entire film was shot at the Twentieh Century-Fox studios, "and the illusion is marvelous," Cronyn said. "Today, it would be done with computerized effects, but Hitchcock pre-

ceded all of this technology, and he did it without the use of those tools, and shot extraordinary things."

Of course people wondered, "Well, where will Hitchcock have his cameo appearance if the entire film is taking place on a lifeboat?" Look for him in a diet ad on the page of a newspaper held by one of the actors. The bigger the problem, as far as Hitchcock was concerned, the better the solution.

ABOVE On the set of *Lifeboat*, clockwise from bottom center: Tallulah Bankhead, John Hodiak, Mary Anderson, Hume Cronyn, and Henry Hull

Hitchcock never lost track of what the story was about, and he communicates it to the audience visually throughout his films in surprising and clever ways. Often some image at the beginning of a film will yield a visual payoff at some point down the storyline. For instance, in his film *Young and Innocent* (1938), and as mentioned earlier, the killer's eyes twitch when he gets nervous. At the end of the film, our heroes end up in a lounge. There is a band on stage, and the killer is a musician playing the drums—but the heroes don't know it. The camera starts tracking from far away and ends on an extreme close-up of the killer's eyes, which are twitching because he knows he is about to get caught. That stretched-out moment builds suspense and makes us part of the story. We're now almost screaming at our heroes to look at the guy on stage. At the same time, we're sharing the villain's sudden anxiety that he is about to be discovered. The whole thing is almost comical because it is so nerve-wracking for the audience—and so manipulative on the part of the director. Hitchcock employs this technique of focusing the audience's attention on an object or a reaction that might seem insignificant on the surface. He uses it to clue us in, telling us to pay attention, that something is about to happen.

In *Notorious* (1946) Ingrid Bergman has stolen the key to the cellar from her husband. She intends to give it to Cary Grant during a party so they can find out what's hidden in the wine cellar. The camera starts as a wide shot on the party from the balcony and comes down slowly to end in a close-up of the key in Ingrid Bergman's nervously clenched fist. The party is just a party—but the shot accentuates the intensity of what the lead character is feeling. Underneath the fun, there's jeopardy. There's a ticking time bomb.

In *Marnie* (1964), Tippi Hedren plays a compulsive thief. She works for someone for a while and then robs money from the safe. One of her latest victims is a man named Strutt. We're introduced to him in one of the first scenes of the movie. In fact, he says the first line of dialogue in the film: "Robbed!" Even though Marnie gets away, Strutt knows who the thief is. Much, much later in the movie, there's a party for which Hitchcock reproduced his tracking shot from *Notorious*, starting from the top of the stairs, then moving down to the front door opening and closing as guests arrive, ending on a close-up of Strutt, the one man who can identify Marnie as a thief. That descent is suspenseful and ratchets up audience anxiety, because we know—we've just been shown—something is about to happen.

Hitchcock never moved his camera gratuitously. There was always a purpose. It was either to keep us in the action or, as in the case of *Frenzy* (1972), to keep us out. At one point in that film, the villain brings a woman home then closes the door as if in our face, while we hear him say, "You're my type of woman." As our imagination starts projecting the horror that is about to happen in the room, the camera tracks down all the way into the street. During that long shot, we have plenty of time to register that another victim has been added to the story. It is almost more violent than if we had been witness to the actual murder, which we later see as a flashback, but in quick, almost subliminal cuts.

Another remarkable scene has to do with Hitchcock embracing the literary idea, from the Daphne du Maurier novel, that we should never see the title character in *Rebecca*. There are no pictures or paintings of her anywhere. Yet we get a vivid por-

trait of her from those who knew her. When we get to the crucial scene where Max de Winter (Laurence Olivier) reveals to his second wife (Joan Fontaine) how Rebecca died (in her bungalow on the beach while taunting her husband, accidentally tripping, falling, and fatally hitting her head), we don't get a flashback, which would have been the more typical way to present it. Instead, the camera pans across the empty room, hitting each of the spots where Rebecca would have been standing as Max tells us exactly what she was saying and doing on that fateful night. Because we have such a strong impression of Rebecca, our imagination vividly pictures her during her last moments and fills in the empty space. In that scene alone, Hitchcock proves that you don't need to show everything—or everyone—in order to evoke a reaction from the audience.

Hitchcock also knew that he could get away with certain things that the audience, once engaged in

the story, would not notice or question. The logic (or lack thereof) to certain plot points in bad movies is often obvious—but in Hitchcock's films, you never question anything because you are so engaged not only with the story, but with the way the story is being told. Same goes with his visuals. You may spot the woman who is riding a horse alongside Claude Rains in an early scene in *Notorious*. When Ingrid Bergman is invited to his house later on, what seems to be the same woman can be spotted entering the dining room and sitting at the table. She is otherwise absent from that particular scene. Although it is pure speculation, it is possible that in the editing process Hitchcock decided that it would be more powerful to feature in the scene only the two women central to the story: Ingrid Bergman and Claude Rains's mother, Madame Sebastian. The point being that the audience never questions the two shots where the woman appears because they are so engaged with the other characters. Hitchcock knew that the strength of their screen presence would allow him to leave in an obvious mistake; that, in essence, no one would notice the woman, at least not on first viewing.

It is fitting to mention here, as well, a couple of bizarre scenes in *Suspicion* (1941). In the first, two detectives come to Lina (Joan Fontaine) and Johnny (Cary Grant's) home to announce the "suspicious" death of the Nigel Bruce character, Beaky. Upon entering the home, one of the police inspectors looks at a small abstract painting on the wall. The man's glance at the piece of art is underlined by a short musical bit. It happens again as he exits the home. In no other scene is the painting highlighted. It's a very short glimpse into a very minor character's own sense of observation. Perhaps Hitchcock himself liked

ABOVE On the set of *Suspicion* (1941)
PAGE 137 With Joan Fontaine, who played the role of Lina in *Suspicion*

HITCHCOCK
piece by piece

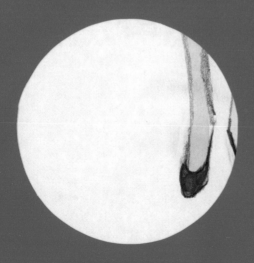

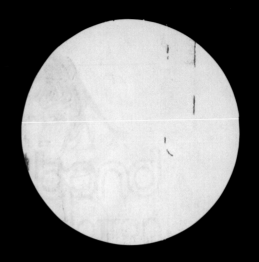

HITCHCOCK
piece by piece

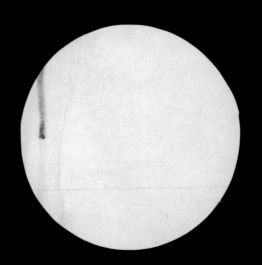

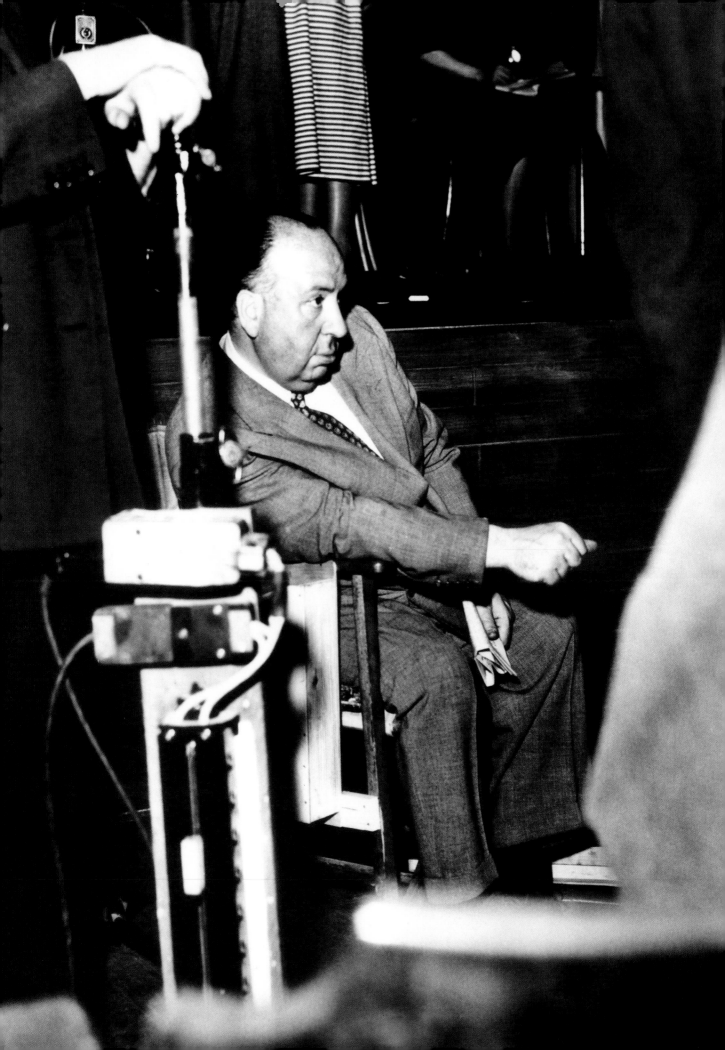

(or disliked) the painting and felt the need to bring our attention to it. Later in the film, Isobel, the local murder mystery writer (played by Auriol Lee) invites Lina and Johnny to a dinner party at her home. At the table are two other guests, Isobel's creepy brother (he is a pathologist, who is seen cutting up his chicken with great precision, as if he was dissecting a body, while discussing the results of an autopsy) and a woman dressed like a man, who is never introduced. In fact, in looking at the censorship correspondence of the time, it was requested of Hitchcock to tone down Johnny's remarks toward the woman, as he jokes about her masculinity. Was the woman with the brother, or was she Isobel's girlfriend? Either way, she is unforgettable and definitely brings to the scene additional dimension and texture as the main characters discuss whether death by poison would be painful, and if Johnny is of the murderous kind.

In that same film, Hitchcock does wonderful things with light, or lack of it. It's fascinating that the film starts in complete darkness. We only hear Johnny speak before we meet him: "Oh, I beg your pardon, was that your leg?" as he enters a compartment while the train is going through a tunnel. Only when the train emerges does daylight reveal both Johnny and Lina. This sets the stage for the two sides of Cary Grant's character: dark and light. The real mystery of the film is discovering which is the real Johnny. Later on, Lina thinks that Johnny may have pushed his friend Beaky over a cliff. As she enters the living room and realizes that Beaky is still alive, the room suddenly becomes brighter (just as Lina takes off her coat), as if a dark veil has been lifted. And toward the conclusion of the film, Hitchcock wanted us to feel real menace coming from Johnny (especially after he

discussed the existence of an untraceable yet deadly poison), when he brings a glass of milk to Lina. To make the audience believe that he may have put poison in the milk, the director had a light bulb placed inside the glass to make it glow.

Hitchcock reprised his glass-of-milk virtuosity (what could be more innocent than a nice glass of milk?) in *Spellbound* (1945). When John Ballantyne (Gregory Peck) is having one of his psychotic episodes, he comes downstairs and is given a glass of milk. To signal to the audience that the milk contained something intended to put the patient to sleep, Hitchcock visually "drowns" us in the glass. A conventional way to do this might have been to film a simple shot of Peck drinking the milk and then fainting to the ground. But by creating the subjective point of view, Hitchcock transitions to the next scene in a clever and surreal manner, which matches the spirit of the sequence that follows, in which Peck's dreams are psychoanalyzed.

Whether he worked in black and white or in color, Hitchcock paid great attention to photography as part of his storytelling. In *Spellbound*, John Ballantyne suffers from amnesia and gets frightened by the color white (he witnessed a man getting murdered on a snow-covered slope). Hitchcock accentuates his phobia on several occasions. Years later, Marnie (Tippi Hedren) would be sensitive to the color red: she killed a man she believed was assaulting her mother, and red, as in the blood on the dead man's white shirt, is what triggers the repressed terror of her tragic past. In that film, Hitchcock tints the entire screen red in order to convey Marnie's phobia; however, he does it in a completely unrealistic fashion. When the camera focuses on the actress as she

LEFT On the set of *Stage Fright* (1950)

is reacting to the color, the shot is tinted in red. Logic would dictate that only her point of view should be red. But instead, Hitchcock makes us one with Marnie for dramatic effect each time her phobia surges. Equally dramatic (albeit of a different nature), is a brief shot in *Lifeboat* where several of the characters are standing facing the camera, but all we can really see is their silhouettes and the whites of their eyes. For a second, with that shot alone, we are no longer watching a war drama, but a horror film. And horror is literally what the characters are experiencing.

While Lina in *Suspicion* may not have had anything to fear in the end—the glass of milk was not poisoned—Alicia (Ingrid Bergman) in *Notorious* is not so lucky. After her husband and his mother have discovered that she is an American agent spying on them, they begin to slowly poison her. In the brilliant and suspenseful scene where Alicia realizes what's happening to her (that her coffee is laced with poison), Hitchcock conveys both the physical and psychological shock of this discovery by tracking in on the guilty parties (Alex Sebastian and then his mother), and then by distorting the image and the

sound. The image seems to float and then turn to a negative. It is a compelling and frightening moment. And earlier, you may notice that Hitchcock placed the coffee cup in the foreground. Could it be in fact an oversized prop? The object seems to overpower the character and the screen, informing us of its lethal aspect. Similarly, in *Rebecca*, each time the second Mrs. de Winter (Joan Fontaine) opens a door, she seems completely dwarfed by the size of it, with the knob always placed much higher than it would normally be found. It may well be that British mansions were designed that way, but only Joan Fontaine seems diminished and overpowered by the doors. Hitchcock's gothic approach reinforces the fact that Maxim's new wife is less than welcomed at Manderley. In *Dial M for Murder* (1954), and as indicated in the title, the telephone is the signal to kill Margot (Grace Kelly). When her husband (Ray Milland) dials his home number in order to wake up his wife (to get her to the perfect spot for a hired killer to strangle her), Hitchcock filmed an oversized finger and dial, again emphasizing suspense by exaggerating our perspective on the phone. In *Spellbound* (1945), when Ingrid Bergman confronts the

ABOVE With Ingrid Bergman on the set of *Spellbound* (1945)
RIGHT Billboard for *Spellbound* in New York City

killer and exits the room, Hitchcock chose to film this completely from the madman's point of view, using a giant hand holding a giant gun—eventually, the gun turns directly to us and fires, with a splash of red flashing in the otherwise black-and-white film.

Dreams play a role in many of Hitchcock's films. The dream sequence of *Spellbound*, although heavily edited in the end, was designed in collaboration with the great surrealist artist Salvador Dali. Hitchcock started *Rebecca*, as in the novel, with a dream narrated by the nameless heroine of the story: "Last night I dreamt I went to Manderley again . . . " And later, Fontaine dreams of her employer, Mrs. Van Hopper, repeating to her over and over how Maxim cannot get over his wife's death. In *Marnie*, clues to the title character's disturbed past are found in recurring nightmares she has. "I was having that old dream again . . ." she tells her mother. "First the tapping . . . and then . . . it's always when you come to the door. That's when the cold starts."

The director would also visit the world of dreams in *Vertigo* (1958). James Stewart's nightmare following the death of Madeleine gives us access to his mind. And like the dream sequence in *Spellbound*, Hitchcock uses symbols—in this case falling images and even animation representing the character's fear of heights—to convey the depth of what Stewart is feeling.

Alfred Hitchcock loved to travel. And he felt that his films, when necessary for storytelling, should bear the mark of a specific locale. Framing the story around a specific place was a clever way to engage audiences with the characters. As we've seen, in *Saboteur* (1942), the fact that the climactic confrontation between the hero and the villain took place on top of the Statue of Liberty tied in with the plot, which revolved around traitors and, in essence, the fight for freedom. In *North by Northwest* (1959), that very same type of confrontation takes place on top of Mount Rushmore—also a fitting location since the movie is about government secrets. *Stage Fright* (1950) is about travesty—the villain is an actor and plays the role of the victim quite convincingly (he is in fact a psychotic killer)—and so, appropriately, the RADA (London's Royal Academy of Dramatic Art) takes center stage in the story. Key elements of *Secret Agent* (1936) take place in Switzerland, so Hitchcock stages a scene inside a chocolate factory. The beginning of *Foreign Correspondent* is set in Holland, so Hitchcock playfully uses windmills as a plot device. Other landmarks indelibly identified with Hitchcock's cinema include the Royal Albert Hall (for both versions of *The Man Who Knew Too Much*), the British Museum (*Blackmail*), the Tower of London (*Frenzy*), and the Golden Gate Bridge (*Vertigo*). Real cities like Bodega Bay (*The Birds*) and the fictional Bates Motel from *Psycho* are also as iconic as the films themselves.

Hitchcock didn't need a historical place marker to make a scene unforgettable. Witness what Hitchcock did in *North by Northwest,* for instance, with a completely deserted road. Cary Grant is waiting there to meet a certain George Kaplan (who doesn't even exist) and ends up being chased by a menacing crop-dusting plane. The sequence relies purely on clever camera angles and, ultimately, editing. What Hitchcock accomplishes here is not only suspense, but also unparalleled action with very few components: just an empty field, a plane, and an actor. A fascinating touch

LEFT Hitchcock in the 1940s

here is Hitchcock's choice not to have any music on the soundtrack until the plane goes out of control, hits a gasoline truck, and explodes.

While undeniably the Master of Suspense, Hitchcock, as we have seen, is also a Master of Romance, and the combination of those two personae (with a healthy dose of humor thrown in) is a recipe for any number of the director's best films. Keep one component out, however, and the famous Hitchcock touch might fumble a bit, as happened with the romantic comedy *Mr. and Mrs. Smith* (1941). In it, a young couple (Carole Lombard and Robert Montgomery) discover they may not be legally married. Fresh from an argument, the couple needs to lose each other before they can find themselves again. The film is extremely charming, but romance and humor are better showcased when they don't take center stage, but rather when they're integrated with suspense.

Very few of Hitchcock's films lack (black) humor. Among them you find his most realistic films, *Lifeboat* (1944), *I Confess* (1953), and *The Wrong Man* (1956). The director used a very serious approach in crafting them. As a result they are much less memorable than many of his other pictures, most of which are notable for their wit and sly jokes, including performances by secondary characters such as Thelma Ritter in *Rear Window* (1954), Jessie Royce Landis in both *North by Northwest* and *To Catch a Thief* (1955), and the cast of Hitch's successful black comedy about a dead body, *The Trouble with Harry* (1955).

Obviously humor is integral to Hitch's make-up, as became clearly evident when the director came in front of the camera to do the introductions to his television series. His roundly intoned greeting, "Good

evening..." was always the promise of a funny speech about death, murder, or other unpleasantness. Hitch had a delivery that inevitably reminded us of the humor and irony hidden behind the grimmest subjects. Even when the director started hosting trailers for his films, like *Psycho, The Birds,* and *Marnie,* he always managed to make us smile, regardless of the situation he was depicting. In talking about what took place in the shower at the Bates Motel in *Psycho,* Hitchcock makes a fuss about "the blood," and how we should have seen it, it was everywhere!

But the director knew that humor worked best when it was combined with tension. There are plenty of examples in Hitchcock's films where audience nervousness gives way to relieved laughter. One favorite example is in the remake of *The Man Who Knew Too Much* (1956), when James Stewart, following a clue in search of his kidnapped son, assumes that "Ambrose Chapel" is a person and not a place, as it turns out to be. He finds himself on "a wild goose chase" at a taxidermist shop. The scene is first suspenseful, with Bernard Herrmann's music accentuating the tension; the shop itself is morbid, and the characters in it look suspicious. But as Stewart realizes he is in the wrong place, the situation lightens up and turns to comedy as our hero has to fight his way out of the shop amid the stuffed animals. In one short sequence, Hitchcock offers two very opposite and separate takes on a situation; one suspenseful and the other comedic.

In *Stage Fright* (1950), Jane Wyman, playing an aspiring actress trying to solve a crime, needs to go undercover as an assistant to Marlene Dietrich. She disguises herself by putting on her mother's thick

RIGHT Publicity picture for the *Alfred Hitchcock Presents* series

glasses, a ridiculous hat, and a dowdy outfit. To complete the picture, she adopts a vulgar manner of smoking and a new accent. She tests her new look on her eccentric mother (Dame Sybil Thorndike), hoping that she won't recognize her, but instead her mother says, "Oh, there you are. Help me find my glasses, Eve, darling. I can't see a thing!" That scene owes as much to Hitchcock as it does to Wyman's impeccable comic timing and body language.

In that same film, you also have the unforgettable and hilarious performance of Alistair Sim, who plays Jane Wyman's father. His bickering with both his daughter and his estranged wife is delicious. Humor helps us realize that, as the director once said, the traditional Hitchcock film "encompasses true horror and comedy at the same time." And, yes, to him, *Psycho* was "a big comedy. It had to be." But perhaps, Hitchcock was *joking* when he made that statement!

It's hard to look away when watching a Hitchcock film. Also it's easy to "hum" Hitchcock, as some of the scores are as famous as the films themselves. Think of the shrieking violins in *Psycho*. Probably the most famous association in Hitchcock's career was with composer Bernard Herrmann, who scored some of the director's best films. Herrmann and Hitchcock first collaborated on *The Trouble with Harry* (1955), for which the composer had to bring a personality to a corpse—the titular Harry, who is found dead at the beginning of the film. The music, as established in the opening credits, tells us that this will not be a grim story, but rather a comedy about a corpse. Eventually, Herrmann would title that particular piece of music, "A Portrait of Hitch." Herrmann's scores would always establish the mood of the film in the opening

credit sequences, whether it be *Vertigo, Marnie, North by Northwest*, or others. Sadly, Hitchcock rejected Herrmann's score for *Torn Curtain* (1966), a decision that ended their working relationship. Portions of that composition would reappear years later in the Martin Scorsese remake of *Cape Fear* (1991), rescored by Elmer Bernstein.

Music was always on Hitchcock's mind, and it sometimes was even part of the plot itself. In *The 39 Steps*, Richard Hannay cannot get a tune out of his head, a tune he heard when he first saw a certain Mr. Memory perform at a music hall. Upon hearing the tune again at the end of the film, Hannay connects the dots back to Mr. Memory and realizes that spies are using him to memorize government secrets. Similarly, in *The Lady Vanishes* (1938), a tune, when played, contains vital information. And isn't it at the crash of the cymbals during a performance of the "Storm Cloud Cantata" that a statesman is to be assassinated in *The Man Who Knew Too Much*? In *Rear Window*, there is a subtle message for James Stewart in the love song that's being written by one of his neighbors, a struggling composer. The full song comes together at the end. It is entitled "Lisa," just like the character played by Grace Kelly, the love interest in the story. It's the melody of a waltz ("The Merry Widow") that Teresa Wright is trying to identify in *Shadow of a Doubt* (1943), as she discovers the truth about her uncle, the killer of elderly widows. The killer in *Young and Innocent* is a musician and is identified at the end of the film as he is performing on stage. Manny Balestrero in *The Wrong Man* is also a musician, and so is Alfred Hitchcock himself in his cameo appearance in *Strangers on a Train* (1951), when he boards a train carrying a double bass. Scenes at a music hall are featured in *The Lodger*

(1927) and *Stage Fright*. And there is a scene reminiscent of *The Man Who Knew Too Much* in *Torn Curtain*: Paul Newman and Julie Andrews are to meet with a contact in order to escape on a ship from East Berlin back to America. They're attending a ballet and Newman screams "Fire!" to create a distraction, as it appears the lead dancer has recognized them and is about to turn them over to the authorities.

Of Hitchcock's sweeping dramatic scores, Bernard Herrmann wasn't the only composer to capture the director's vision through music. There was Franz Waxman, who wrote the remarkable and haunting scores for *Rebecca*, *The Paradine Case* (1947), and *Rear Window*; Dimitri Tiomkin, for *Dial M for Murder* and *Strangers on a Train*; Miklós Rózsa, who won an Oscar for his innovative score for *Spellbound*; Ron Goodwin, who did the music for *Frenzy* (replacing Henry Mancini), and others, including John Williams, who scored Hitchcock's last film, *Family Plot* (1976).

Williams had just done *Jaws* (another "catchy" score) in 1975, and through the head of the music department at Universal (a man named Harry Garfield), he was introduced to Hitchcock. As usual, there was a brief meeting at the studio. The next day, Williams learned he was hired. In later years, the composer of scores for so many classic films described his experience working with the Master of Suspense as very professional. They'd watch the film together, and Hitch would indicate where there should be music and where there shouldn't be music (in technical terms, *spotting sessions*). Williams recalled a particularly insightful conversation with Hitchcock. Apparently on one of his most recent films, Hitch had worked with a composer who had scored a murder scene

with predictable—but adequate—lugubrious sounds. It was not what Hitchcock wanted. When John Williams asked his director why, Hitchcock simply replied, "Mr. Williams, murder can be fun!"

Because Hitchcock had started making movies in the silent era, there is a sense that he understood to a greater degree, perhaps over directors who came afterward, the potential power of a soundtrack—as if a mute had suddenly been given the ability to speak. This is apparent from his first talkie, *Blackmail* (1929).The heroine, played by Anny Ondra, has stabbed and killed a man in self-defense. The next day news of the crime is everywhere. She is at a table and asked to cut a slice of bread while a neighbor tells everyone present about the murder. But all we hear is each time the neighbor says the word *knife*. The rest of her dialogue is garbled. The poor girl responsible for the killing is hesitant in handling the knife at the table and eventually drops it when the neighbor delivers one last and loud "… knife!"

Then there's the unforgettable scream from the female lead during a concert at the Albert Hall in *The Man Who Knew Too Much*, meant to interrupt a murder. Screams of course are a trademark of anything scary—Janet Leigh in *Psycho* is a good example, as is the anticipation of the scream in *Frenzy* as a secretary returns to her office; we know she is about to discover that her boss has been strangled, but Hitchcock keeps his camera outside, on the street. We wait and wait until, to our great relief, we hear the horrifying scream. But Hitch sometimes used prosaic sounds to provide suspense, as in an amazing sequence in *Torn Curtain* where Paul Newman, aware that he is being followed, tries to

lose his tail by going into a museum. All we hear are footsteps sounding against the marble floors of the galleries. Hitchcock in that scene creates a score using only the sound of footsteps. The pacing of the sound alone is what drives the action and suspense. Later, silence is just as important when Newman is "forced" to kill Gromek (Wolfgang Kieling), the agent who is on to him. The murder takes place in a kitchen, and in order not to alert the taxi driver waiting outside, Newman has to try his best to keep the man from screaming. He and a woman end up dragging Gromek on the floor and shoving his head inside a gas oven. It's really the struggle to keep the man silent that creates the suspense.

Hitchcock also used sound to mark a narrative transition, as in the case of *The 39 Steps*. In that film, a landlady finds the corpse of a woman who has been stabbed. She turns to the camera, and as she screams, we immediately cut to the loud whistling of a train leaving the station (and on board is Richard Hannay, the man who will be wrongly accused of the crime). In *Young and Innocent*, two women discover the lifeless body of a victim washed ashore. As they're about to scream, Hitchcock cuts to the sound of seagulls above—an ominous foreshadowing of *The Birds*.

In Hitchcockian terms, there are such things as silent screams, as demonstrated in *The Birds*. Jessica Tandy, who plays Rod Taylor's mother, goes to visit a neighboring farmer. She enters his house, notices that all of the cups that hang on hooks in the kitchen have been broken (only the handles remain). She goes to the back of the house, toward the bedroom, and finds the poor man dead. The instinct here would have been to have her scream, but Hitchcock knows better. Instead, she runs out of the house, completely unable to make a sound. It's as if the scream is strangled in her throat. And it is we, in our seats, who want to scream because the absence of it on the soundtrack is so potent!

In *Marnie*, the heroine is a kleptomaniac. In the scene where she is about to rob the safe of her boss after office hours, she initially hides in a bathroom stall. Rather than showing us people leaving, Hitch focuses on Marnie listening to voices of colleagues walking away until complete silence indicates to her she can come out. As Marnie empties the safe, Hitchcock shows us the adjoining corridor where a cleaning woman has started washing the floors. Marnie puts her shoes in her coat pockets and tiptoes out of the office, keeping an eye on the woman. Then the camera shows us that one of the shoes is about to fall. Suddenly it hits the floor loudly. The cleaning woman has no reaction, though, because she is deaf! Brilliant suspense and humor and irony—Hitch leaves it to us, the audience, to provide our own soundtrack as we scream to Marnie, warning her that her shoe is about to fall.

In *Frenzy*, Hitchcock elects to set his camera outside the glass doors of a tribunal, preventing us from hearing Richard Blaney's trial, except when someone opens the door. Hitchcock only wanted us to hear the result of the trial (Blaney is pronounced guilty), and the director stretched out the moment through the way he established the scene. Hitchcock's clever and suspenseful solution makes us voyeurs to the scene (wanting to hear more) rather than passive witnesses to it.

Climactic endings were also a Hitchcock trademark, and some were more spectacular than others. We've

LEFT On the set of *Strangers on a Train* (1951)

already highlighted *Saboteur* and *North by Northwest*, talked about the different endings designed for *Suspicion* and *Topaz*, and the ironic conclusions of *Frenzy* ("Mr. Rusk, you're not wearing your tie . . .") and *To Catch a Thief* ("Oh, Mother will love it up here!"), among others. But there's the breathtaking train crash in *Secret Agent* (1936), and although done completely with miniatures, it is an incredible technical achievement for its time.

Another of the best Hitchcockian climactic action sequences is at the end of *Foreign Correspondent* (1940). Credit is to be given to production designer and second unit director William Cameron Menzies for his contribution to the scene. It shows the result of an amazing collaboration between all the departments involved with the realization of a plane crashing into the sea. Hitchcock decided to show it from the point of view of the pilots. In front of them is a screen. Projected onto it is a shot heading toward the water. On the moment of impact, gallons of water were poured from behind the screen. If you watch that scene frame by frame, you see the water literally ripping the screen apart.

Later in Hitchcock's career, there's the final confrontation between Farley Granger and Robert Walker in *Strangers on a Train,* which takes place on a merry-go-round gone out of control. The drama contained in that sequence engages the audience through several perspectives, but purely from a cinematic angle, imagine the excitement of seeing that sequence in the forties!

The visuals, the cast, the great scripts, the photography, the camera angles, the unforgettable shots, the cameo appearances, the specific themes, the scores,

the editorial choices . . . all these elements, as we've seen, combine to constitute the Hitchcock Touch. But beyond the filmmaker's cinematic and storytelling brilliance, there are other elements that make his work uniquely Hitchcockian, including the director's idiosyncratic attachment to certain things that he enjoyed hanging his plots and characters on, like trains and keys. One such personal passion of the director's, above all, of course, is his great preoccupation off- and on-screen: food.

"A few years ago, in Santa Rosa, California, I caught a side view of myself in a store window and screamed with fright," Hitchcock once said about his rather corpulent figure. "Since then, I limit myself to a three-course dinner of appetizer, fish, and meat, with only one bottle of vintage wine with each course." On another occasion, he said, "It's been my observation that a man does not live by murder alone. He needs affection, approval, encouragement, and, occasionally, a hearty meal." Food was as abundant in his films as it was on his table. The Hitchcocks would in fact bring their own cook to Hollywood. They imported English bacon and Dover sole, which was kept in storage at the Los Angeles Smoking and Curing Company. His favorite restaurant in Hollywood was Chasen's, where he would usually order a double steak and a champagne punch made according to his own specifications.

This fascination with food made it to the screen. Hitchcock loved to show his characters eating and discussing food, but his own commentary on the subject was best. He once said, "I do not believe in raw sex. I like my sex cooked, preferably with a delicate sauce." This applied both to his culinary predilection as well as his preference for visuals revealing seduc-

PAGE 153 Hitchcock in his wine cellar at home in Bel Air, California, 1974

HITCHCOCK
piece by piece

tion, marriage, relationship, and murder. His gastronomic sensibility also extended to the graphic nature of violence, as evidenced in his observation that, "There will obviously be a lot of drama in the steak that is too rare."

In *Rear Window*, Grace Kelly is often cooking or bringing food to James Stewart—her way of suggesting he should marry her. There is a similar scene in *Notorious* where Ingrid Bergman invites Cary Grant for dinner, hinting at how wonderful it is to eat in style and how, once married, it must happen every day. But it's also over food that, in *Rear Window*, Stewart and Thelma Ritter discuss murder and the neighbor across the way. Since we haven't witnessed any crime, the only reaction we get from the gruesome, speculative details spelled out by Thelma Ritter is through watching James Stewart lose his appetite.

The most celebrated and seductive line in a Hitchcock film may be in *To Catch a Thief*, when Grace Kelly innocently (or perhaps not so) asks Cary Grant over a picnic basket, "Do you want a leg or a breast?" His answer is simple: "You choose." A similar conversation is featured between Eva Marie Saint and Grant in *North by Northwest* as he sits across from her in a dining car on a train and she declares that she never discusses love on an empty stomach. Later, when they're kissing in the train compartment, their exchange has to do with Cary Grant having taste in food, clothes, and women. He concludes, "I like your flavor."

Rope is completely centered on a meal served on a chest in which a murder victim is hidden. Placing candlesticks on the chest, one of the killers proudly observes that they "suggest a ceremonial altar" from which the guests (including the family, friends, and girlfriend of the dead man) will be eating "our sacrificial feast." Later on it is mentioned that Farley Granger's character, the other killer, is quite good at strangling chickens!

A discussion of death and murder takes place at the table in *Suspicion, Strangers on a Train, To Catch a Thief,* and others, including *Frenzy,* in which the wife of the detective in charge of the necktie murders experiments with (mostly repulsive-looking) nouvelle cuisine throughout the film, adding a layer of humor to the progress of the investigation. The killer, Bob Rusk, played by Barry Foster, works at a fruit market and hides one of the bodies in a potato bag. He later has to go retrieve a piece of evidence (his tie pin), which the victim grabbed when she was being strangled inside the potato truck.

And of course, food is on the menu in *Psycho,* from the first scene, where Janet Leigh and John Gavin meet to have sex during her lunch hour, to her last meal with Norman Bates—a simple sandwich and a glass of milk—during which he observes she eats like a bird. And later, it's in the fruit cellar that Mrs. Bates's corpse is found.

In *Rebecca*, Mrs. Danvers terrorizes the second Mrs. de Winter by asking her to fill in blank space on a menu with suggestions for sauces. In *The Paradine Case,* Lord Horfield, played by Charles Laughton, observes on one hand that Ann Todd is very appetizing ("A charming compliment coming from a gourmet such as yourself," she comments back to him) and later, after he has made the decision to give the death penalty to Mrs. Paradine (for poisoning her husband), he observes how "closely the convolutions of a walnut resemble those of the human brain." Part of the plot of the second version of *The Man Who Knew Too Much* unfolds in a restaurant in Morocco, with James Stewart being unable to eat the local food properly.

Hitchcock declared he hated eggs. No surprise then, that Jessie Royce Landis puts out a cigarette in an egg dish in *To Catch a Thief*. There is also a suggestion in *The Birds* that birds are getting their revenge on mankind because we've been eating them! His trailer for *The Birds* began with Hitchcock eating chicken. Similarly, he introduced *Frenzy* by standing in front of a bag of potatoes. Then he opens the bag and a woman's leg springs out of it. "I've heard of a leg of lamb, a leg of chicken, but never of a leg of potatoes," the director says nonchalantly. The examples of food in Hitchcock's films go on. This systematic and almost compulsive inclusion of something as common as food in cinema was, on Hitchcock's part, another device to engage his audience with his plots and characters. A way to whet our appetite and keep our attention alert and on edge. A way to keep us wanting more, coming back, and asking for seconds.

Other Hitchcock patterns, as observed in *Les Cahiers du Cinéma* in the late 1950s, include handcuffs, which first appeared in *The Lodger* (1927). Later, in *The 39 Steps* and *Saboteur*, not only did handcuffs literally remind us that the heroes of both stories were accused men on the run, but also they were used by Hitchcock to create sexual tension between the "wrong man" and the girl he is traveling with. In *The 39 Steps*, Pamela (Madeleine Carroll) is removing her stockings while Richard Hannay (Robert Donat) is enjoying running his own hand up and down her legs, and because they're handcuffed to one another,

he doesn't have to apologize for his intimate caresses! Pamela, who has no clue how much the presumed killer is enjoying being attached to her, asks Hannay to hold her sandwich while she continues taking off her stockings. In *Saboteur*, Barry Kane (Robert Cummings) tries to saw off his handcuffs on a car's running engine belt, while Pat Martin (Priscilla Lane) is trying to escape from him. Eventually, Barry manages to catch her before she can really call out for help and shoves her back inside the car, kicking and screaming as an elderly couple driving by concludes that the young couple must be terribly in love!

Keys are also important and recurring objects. They mean suspense in *Dial M for Murder*, *Notorious*, *Under Capricorn*, and *Marnie*. Rings, as in *Rear Window* and *Shadow of a Doubt*, or jewelry and diamonds, as in *Saboteur*, *Notorious*, *Lifeboat*, *To Catch a Thief*, and *Family Plot*, or even the tiepin in *Frenzy* are essential plot points and are used as ways to define characters and to elicit tension.

Hitchcock uses the glasses worn by the victim in *Strangers on a Train* to stage one of his most memorable murder scenes: the killing is reflected in the glasses after they fall to the ground during the victim's fruitless struggle against her attacker. The brilliance of this device makes the scene visually memorable. By designing these exciting shots, by including specific objects, Hitchcock makes us watch and pay attention; under other circumstances, we may have looked away during the murder. Another significant object in that film that relates to the murder is a lighter that belongs to Guy Haines (Farley Granger). He forgets it on the train after meeting Bruno Anthony (Robert Walker). Bruno is about to return it to Guy, but hesitates and keeps it. Before

Bruno strangles Miriam, he ignites the lighter to illuminate her face and later on, he plans to plant the lighter at the scene of the crime to incriminate Guy. Oddly, one of the most suspenseful scenes of that film has us rooting for Bruno when he inadvertently drops the lighter in a drain. We almost want him to get it back! Hitchcock is *that* clever in his manipulation of suspense. Doesn't matter what side we're on, we can't help but cringe as Bruno's hand slides through the iron bars to reach down the drain for the lighter and wish for his fingers to snap the object up. The other wonderful thing about the lighter is that it's the constant link between Guy and Bruno. On a symbolic level, it hints at the fact that Bruno is Guy's dark side. On a practical level, the lighter means the difference in the appearance of guilt or innocence.

Trains and train stations are integral to the drama and take center stage of many key sequences in Hitchcock's best films, from *Number Seventeen* (1932) to *The 39 Steps, Secret Agent, The Lady Vanishes, Suspicion, Shadow of a Doubt, Spellbound, The Paradine Case, North by Northwest, Marnie*, and, of course, *Strangers on a Train*. Hitch also stages scenes in subways in *The Wrong Man* and *Blackmail*.

Trains are perfect settings for seduction. We've mentioned the obvious symbol of the train entering the tunnel at the end of *North by Northwest* and the curious encounter between Cary Grant and Joan Fontaine aboard a train while it's going through a tunnel in *Suspicion*. It's not much of a stretch to interpret the opening of the story of *Strangers on a Train,* where Bruno Anthony (Robert Walker) tries to convince Guy Haines (Farley Granger) into swapping murders, as a twisted seduction scene.

Hitchcock himself made several of his cameos on a train (*Shadow of a Doubt*), on a subway (*Blackmail*), climbing aboard a train (*Strangers on a Train*), or at a train station (*The Paradine Case*). But the point really is that Hitchcock uses trains as a dramatic arena, one that symbolizes his storytelling skills, one that takes us methodically from one point to another.

Very few filmmakers can claim to be a brand name. Hitchcock was, is, and always will be a *brand*. In his own time, there were of course the filmmaker's successful television shows *(Alfred Hitchcock Presents, The Alfred Hitchcock Hour,* etc.). There were books of short stories bearing his name, music albums even. And it would have been interesting to see what the director would have done today with the advent of new media, sophisticated special effects, and technology. But what distinguished Hitchcock and what would set him apart from other directors even today, was the ability he had to tell compelling stories with fascinating characters and to create a world not only within each film but one that eventually was linked to the different movies he made. You can look at each individual title or at them all as a group, but either way, Hitchcock's oeuvre takes on meaning that comprises a fascinating and unique cinematic universe. François Truffaut said: "When I direct a movie, I realize if I'm having problems with a scene, I always find a solution if I think of Hitchcock." No doubt every filmmaker is indebted to Hitchcock and as audience members, so are we. To paraphrase Truffaut, if you're having problems with a film you're watching, you can always find solace in revisiting a Hitchcock movie. No doubt it will remind you how far reaching the art of cinema can be.

LEFT Publicity picture for the *Alfred Hitchcock Presents* series

conclusion

After Hitchcock did *Family Plot*, there was discussion about making a film called *The Short Night*. Hilton A. Green, a longtime collaborator of Hitchcock's, was very much involved with the development of the project—he even went with Robert Boyle to Europe looking for locations. But one day Green received a call from Hitch's secretary telling him that the director wanted to see him, and that it was very important. "I dropped everything and went to his office," Hilton Green recalled. "And it was just the two of us. He was behind his desk, and he almost had tears in his eyes. And he said, 'I can't go on. I can't make this picture and I would like you to do a favor for me...'" He asked Green to break the news to Lew Wasserman at Universal. Hitch couldn't face him. "I'll never forget calling Mr. Wasserman and telling him that Mr. Hitchcock was retiring. It was a horrible moment for me and it was very tough for Mr. Wasserman, too."

I was still living in France when Alfred Hitchcock died on April 29, 1980. Within the month following his death, all of his films, including his early British pictures, were re-released in small Parisian theatres. I went to all of them. And it was fascinating to identify how each one of his films was an extension of the next, how the themes emerged so neatly, how clearly they all came from the same mind. How gratifying that writing about Hitchcock and discussing him for various books and documentaries has been part of my professional life since 1993. And it has been a great honor and privilege to get to know the master through his collaborators, his family, and through people who either knew him or studied his art. I am forever grateful to Pat Hitchcock O'Connell

and her daughters, Mary Stone, Katie Fiala, and Tere Carrubba. And to (in alphabetical order):

In front of the camera: Diane Baker, Karen Black, Veronica Cartwright, Hume Cronyn, Georgine Darcy, Bruce Dern, William Devane, Laura Elliott, Jon Finch, Joan Fontaine, John Forsythe, Barry Foster, Farley Granger, Tippi Hedren, Martin Landau, Louise Latham, Janet Leigh, Norman Lloyd, Anna Massey, Sylvia Sidney, Rod Taylor, Teresa Wright.

Behind the scenes: Jay Presson Allen, Saul Bass, Robert Bloch, Robert Boyle, Henry Bumstead, Herbert Coleman, Whitfield Cook, Arthur Laurens, Hilton A. Green, Evan Hunter, Howard G. Kazanjian, Rita Riggs, Anthony Shaffer, Joseph Stefano, John Williams.

And to filmmakers such as Peter Bogdanovich, Michael Crichton, Brian De Palma, William Friedkin, Curtis Hanson, and many others, who have shared their own knowledge, passion, and understanding of the master's films and have inspired me to forge my own opinion and point of view on Hitchcock's work.

Some of the observations in this book are things I discovered many years ago. Others I only just noticed recently, proving that despite multiple viewings, Hitchcock's films continue to reveal themselves. But nothing definitive can ever be written about Hitchcock's films—and I know I've only scratched the surface, so I hope this book has inspired you to go back and either discover or re-discover Hitchcock's cinema, to look beyond the image and make your own observations. Orson Welles once said: "Hitchcock is an incredible director." And indeed he was, is, and always will be.

RIGHT Hitchcock at home, 1974

filmography

The dates indicate the years in which the movies were released.

The British Years

Silent Films

1922 *Number Thirteen*
(Wardour & F; unfinished)
Directed and produced by Alfred
Hitchcock. Starring: Clare Greet, Ernest
Thesiger.

1925 *The Pleasure Garden*
(a Gainsborough-Emelka Picture)
Directed by Alfred Hitchcock. Produced
by Michael Balcon. Screenplay by Eliot
Stannard, based on the novel by Oliver
Sandys. Starring: Virginia Valli, Carmelita
Geraghty, Miles Mander.

1927 *The Mountain Eagle*
(a Gainsborough-Emelka Picture)
Directed by Alfred Hitchcock. Produced
by Michael Balcon. Screenplay by Eliot
Stannard. Starring: Bernard Goetzke, Nita
Naldi, Malcolm Keen.

1927 *The Lodger: A Story of the London Fog*
(a Gainsborough Picture)
Directed by Alfred Hitchcock. Produced
by Michael Balcon. Screenplay by Eliot
Stannard, based on the novel *The Lodger*
by Marie Belloc Lowndes. Starring: Ivor
Novello, Malcolm Keen, June.

1927 *Downhill*
(released in the United States as *When
Boys Leave Home*; a Gainsborough
Picture)
Directed by Alfred Hitchcock. Produced
by Michael Balcon. Screenplay by Eliot
Stannard, based on the play by David
LeStrange (pseudonym for Ivor Novello
and Constance Collier). Starring: Ivor
Novello, Robin Irvine, Lillian Braithwaite.

1927 *Easy Virtue*
(a Gainsborough Picture)
Directed by Alfred Hitchcock. Produced
by Michael Balcon. Screenplay by Eliot
Stannard, based on the play by Noel
Coward. Starring: Isabel Jeans, Ian
Hunter, Robin Irvine.

1927 *The Ring*
(a British International Picture)
Directed by Alfred Hitchcock. Produced
by John Maxwell. Screenplay by Alfred
Hitchcock. Starring: Carl Brisson, Lillian
Hall-Davis, Ian Hunter.

1928 *The Farmer's Wife*
(a British International Picture)
Directed by Alfred Hitchcock. Produced
by John Maxwell. Screenplay by Alfred
Hitchcock, based on the play by Eden
Philpotts. Starring: Jameson Thomas,
Lillian Hall-Davis, Gordon Harker.

1928 *Champagne*
(a British International Picture)
Directed by Alfred Hitchcock. Produced
by John Maxwell. Adaptation by Alfred
Hitchcock, based on an original story by
Walter C. Mycroft. Starring: Betty Balfour,
Jean Bradin, Ferdinand Von Alten.

1929 *The Manxman*
(a British International Picture)
Directed by Alfred Hitchcock. Produced
by John Maxwell. Screenplay by Eliot
Stannard, based on the novel by Hall
Caine. Starring: Carl Brisson, Malcolm
Keen, Anny Ondra.

Sound Films

1929 *Blackmail*
(a British International Picture)
Directed by Alfred Hitchcock. Produced
by John Maxwell. Screenplay by Alfred
Hitchcock, based on the play by Charles
Bennett. Dialogue by Benn Levy. Starring:
Anny Ondra (voice: Joan Barry), John
Longden, Donald Calthrop, Cyril Ritchard.

1930 *Elstree Calling*
(a British International Picture)
Directed by Alfred Hitchcock, André
Charlot, Jack Hulbert, Adrian Bunel, and
Paul Murray. Screenplay by Adrian Bunel,
Walter C. Mycroft, and Val Valentine.
Starring: Tommy Handley, Jack Hulbert,
Anna May Wong, Donald Calthrop.

1930 *Juno and the Paycock*
(a British International Picture)
Directed by Alfred Hitchcock. Produced
by John Maxwell. Adaptation by Alfred
Hitchcock and Alma Reville, based on
the play by Sean O'Casey. Starring: Sara
Allgood, Edward Chapman, Maire O'Neill.

1930 *Murder!*
(a British International Picture)
Directed by Alfred Hitchcock. Produced
by John Maxwell. Adaptation by Alfred
Hitchcock and Walter Mycroft, based
on the novel and the play *Enter Sir John*
by Clemence Dane and Helen Simpson.
Starring: Norah Baring, Herbert Marshall,
Miles Mander.

1931 *The Skin Game*
(a British International Picture)
Directed by Alfred Hitchcock. Produced
by John Maxwell. Screenplay by Alma
Reville, based on the play by John
Galsworthy. Starring: C. V. France, Helen
Haye, Edmund Gwenn.

1932 *Number Seventeen*
(a British International Picture)
Directed by Alfred Hitchcock. Produced
by John Maxwell. Screenplay by Alma
Reville, Alfred Hitchcock, and Rodney
Ackland, based on the play by J. Jefferson
Fargeon. Starring: Leon M. Lion, Anne
Grey, John Stuart.

1932 *Rich and Strange*
(released in the United States as *East of
Shanghai*; a British International Picture)
Directed by Alfred Hitchcock. Produced
by John Maxwell. Adaptation by Alfred
Hitchcock. Screenplay by Alma Reville.
Additional dialogue: Val Valentine.
Starring: Henry Kendall, Joan Barry,
Percy Marmont.

1933 *Waltzes from Vienna*
(released in the United States as *Strauss'
Great Waltz*; a Tom Arnold Production)
Directed by Alfred Hitchcock. Produced
by Tom Arnold. Screenplay by Alma
Reville and Guy Bolton, based on the play
by Guy Bolton. Starring: Jessie Matthews,
Esmond Knight, Edmund Gwenn.

1934 *The Man Who Knew Too Much*
(a Gaumont-British Picture)
Directed by Alfred Hitchcock. Produced
by Michael Balcon. Screenplay by Edwin
Greenwood and A. R. Rawlinson, based
on a story by Charles Bennett and D. B.
Wyndham Lewis. Additional dialogue by
Emlyn Williams. Starring: Leslie Banks,
Edna Best, Nova Pilbeam, Peter Lorre,
Frank Vosper, Pierre Fresnay.

1935 *The 39 Steps*
(a Gaumont-British Picture)
Directed by Alfred Hitchcock. Produced
by Michael Balcon. Adaptation by
Charles Bennett, based on the novel
The Thirty-Nine Steps by John Buchan.
Dialogue by Ian Hay. Starring: Robert
Donat, Madeleine Carroll, Lucie
Mannheim, Godfrey Tearle, John Laurie,
Peggy Ashcroft.

1936 *Secret Agent*
(a Gaumont-British Picture)
Directed by Alfred Hitchcock. Produced

by Ivor Montagu. Screenplay by Charles Bennett, from the play by Campbell Dixon, based on stories by W. Somerset Maugham. Dialogue by Ian Hay and Jesse Lasky, Jr. Starring: John Gielgud, Madeleine Carroll, Peter Lorre.

1936 *Sabotage*
(released in the United States as *The Woman Alone*; a Gaumont-British Picture) Directed by Alfred Hitchcock. Produced by Michael Balcon. Screenplay by Charles Bennett, based on the novel *The Secret Agent* by Joseph Conrad. Dialogue by Ian Hay and Helen Simpson. Starring: Sylvia Sidney, Oscar Homolka, Desmond Tester, John Loder, Joyce Barbour.

1938 *Young and Innocent*
(released in the United States as *The Girl Was Young*; a Gaumont-British Picture) Directed by Alfred Hitchcock. Produced by Edward Black. Screenplay by Charles Bennett, Edwin Greenwood, and Anthony Armstrong, based on the novel *A Shilling for Candles* by Josephine Tey. Dialogue by Gerald Savory. Starring: Nova Pilbeam, Derrick de Marney, Percy Marmont, John Longden, George Curzon, Basil Radford, Pamela Carme.

1938 *The Lady Vanishes*
(a Gaumont-British Picture) Directed by Alfred Hitchcock. Produced by Edward Black. Screenplay by Sydney Gilliat and Frank Lauder, based on the novel *The Wheel Spins* by Ethel Lina White. Starring: Margaret Lockwood, Michael Redgrave, Dame May Whitty, Paul Lukas, Cecil Parker, Linden Travers, Naunton Wayne, Basil Radford.

1939 *Jamaica Inn*
(an Erich Pommer Production) Directed by Alfred Hitchcock. Produced by Erich Pommer. Screenplay by Sydney Gilliat and Joan Harrison, based on the novel by Daphne du Maurier. Additional dialogue by J. B. Priestley. Starring: Charles Laughton, Maureen O'Hara, Leslie Banks.

The American Years

1940 *Rebecca*
(a Selznick International Picture) Directed by Alfred Hitchcock. Produced by David O. Selznick. Screenplay by Robert E. Sherwood and Joan Harrison, based on the novel by Daphne du Maurier. Adaptation by Philip MacDonald and Michael Hogan. Starring: Laurence Olivier, Joan Fontaine, Judith Anderson, George Sanders, Florence Bates, Nigel Bruce, Gladys Cooper.

1940 *Foreign Correspondent*
(a Wanger Production; distributed by United Artists) Directed by Alfred Hitchcock. Produced by Walter Wanger. Screenplay by Charles Bennett and Joan Harrison. Dialogue by James Hilton and Robert Benchley. Starring: Joel McCrea, Laraine Day, Herbert Marshall, George Sanders, Albert Basserman, Robert Benchley, Edmund Gwenn.

1941 *Mr. and Mrs. Smith*
(an RKO Radio Picture) Directed by Alfred Hitchcock. Produced by Harry E. Edington. Story and screenplay by Norman Krasna. Starring: Carole Lombard, Robert Montgomery, Gene Raymond.

1941 *Suspicion*
(an RKO Radio Picture) Directed by Alfred Hitchcock. Produced by Harry E. Edington. Screenplay by Samson Raphaelson, Joan Harrison, and Alma Reville, based on the novel *Before the Facts* by Francis Isles. Starring: Joan Fontaine, Cary Grant, Sir Cedric Hardwicke, Dame May Whitty, Nigel Bruce, Auriol Lee, Leo G. Carroll, Heather Angel.

1942 *Saboteur*
(a Frank Lloyd Production for Universal Pictures) Directed by Alfred Hitchcock. Produced by Frank Lloyd. Screenplay by Peter Viertel, Joan Harrison, and Dorothy Parker. Starring: Robert Cummings, Priscilla Lane, Otto Kruger, Alma Kruger, Norman Lloyd.

1943 *Shadow of a Doubt*
(a Jack H. Skirball Production for Universal Pictures) Directed by Alfred Hitchcock. Produced by Jack H. Skirball. Screenplay by Thornton Wilder, Sally Benson, and Alma Reville, based on an original story by Gordon McDonell. Starring: Joseph Cotten, Teresa Wright, Macdonald Carey, Patricia Collinge, Henry Travers, Hume Cronyn, Edna May Wonacott, Charles Bates.

1944 *Lifeboat*
(a 20th Century-Fox Picture) Directed by Alfred Hitchcock. Produced by Kenneth Macgowan. Screenplay by Jo Swerling, based on a story by John Steinbeck. Starring: Tallulah Bankhead, John Hodiak, William Bendix, Hume Cronyn, Walter Slezak.

1945 *Spellbound*
(a Selznick International Picture) Directed by Alfred Hitchcock. Produced by David O. Selznick. Screenplay by Ben Hecht, based on the novel *The House of Dr. Edwardes* by Francis Beeding. Adaptation by Angus MacPhail. Starring: Ingrid Bergman, Gregory Peck, Leo G. Carroll, Norman Lloyd, Michael Chekhov, John Emery.

1946 *Notorious*
(an RKO Radio Picture) Directed and produced by Alfred Hitchcock. Screenplay by Ben Hecht. Starring: Ingrid Bergman, Cary Grant, Claude Rains, Leopoldine Konstantin, Louis Calhern, Ivan Triesault.

1947 *The Paradine Case*
(a David O. Selznick/Vanguard Film) Directed by Alfred Hitchcock. Produced by David O. Selznick. Screenplay by David O. Selznick, based on the novel by Robert Hichens. Adaptation by Alma Reville. Starring: Gregory Peck, Ann Todd, Valli, Charles Laughton, Louis Jourdan, Ethel Barrymore, Charles Coburn, Joan Tetzel, Leo G. Carroll.

1948 *Rope*
(a Transatlantic Picture released by Warner Brothers) Directed by Alfred Hitchcock. Produced by Alfred Hitchcock and Sidney Bernstein. Adaptation by Hume Cronyn, based on the play by Patrick Hamilton. Screenplay by Arthur Laurents. Starring: James Stewart, John Dall, Farley Granger, Sir Cedric Hardwicke, Constance Collier, Joan Chandler.

1949 *Under Capricorn*
(a Transatlantic Picture released by Warner Brothers) Directed by Alfred Hitchcock. Produced by Alfred Hitchcock and Sidney Bernstein. Adaptation by Hume Cronyn. Screenplay by James Bridie, from the play by John Colton and Margaret Linden, based on the novel by Helen Simpson. Starring: Ingrid Bergman, Joseph Cotten, Michael Wilding, Margaret Leighton, Cecil Parker.

1950 *Stage Fright*
(a Warner Brothers-First National
Picture production)
Directed and produced by Alfred
Hitchcock. Screenplay by Whitfield
Cook, based on the novel *Man Running*
by Selwyn Jepson. Adaptation by Alma
Reville. Additional dialogue by James
Bridie. Starring: Jane Wyman, Marlene
Dietrich, Michael Wilding, Richard Todd,
Alastair Sim, Sybil Thorndike, Patricia
Hitchcock, Kay Walsh.

1951 *Strangers on a Train*
(a Warner Brothers-First National
Picture production)
Directed and produced by Alfred
Hitchcock. Adaptation by Whitfield Cook.
Screenplay by Raymond Chandler and
Czenzi Ormonde, based on the novel by
Patricia Highsmith. Starring: Robert
Walker, Farley Granger, Ruth Roman,
Patricia Hitchcock, Laura Elliot, Leo G.
Carroll, Marion Lorne.

1953 *I Confess*
(a Warner Brothers-First National
Picture production)
Directed and produced by Alfred
Hitchcock. Screenplay by George Tabori
and William Archibald, based on the novel
Nos Deux Consciences by Paul Anthelme.
Starring: Montgomery Clift, Anne Baxter,
Karl Malden, Brian Aherne, O. E. Hasse.

1954 *Dial M for Murder*
(a Warner Brothers-First National
Picture production)
Directed and produced by Alfred
Hitchcock. Screenplay by Frederick
Knott, based on his play. Starring: Grace
Kelly, Ray Milland, Robert Cummings,
Anthony Dawson, John Williams.

1954 *Rear Window*
(a Paramount Picture)
Directed and produced by Alfred
Hitchcock. Screenplay by John Michael
Hayes, based on the short story by Cornell
Woolrich. Starring: James Stewart, Grace
Kelly, Thelma Ritter, Wendell Corey,
Raymond Burr, Judith Evelyn.

1955 *To Catch a Thief*
(a Paramount Picture)
Directed and produced by Alfred
Hitchcock. Screenplay by John Michael
Hayes, based on the novel by David Dodge.
Starring: Cary Grant, Grace Kelly, Jessie
Royce Landis, John Williams, Brigitte
Auber, Charles Vanel.

1955 *The Trouble With Harry*
(a Paramount Picture)
Directed and produced by Alfred
Hitchcock. Screenplay by John Michael
Hayes, based on the novel by J. Trevor
Story. Starring: Edmund Gwenn, John
Forsythe, Shirley MacLaine, Mildred
Natwick, Jerry Mathers.

1956 *The Man Who Knew Too Much*
(a Paramount Picture)
Directed by Alfred Hitchcock. Produced
by Alfred Hitchcock and Herbert
Coleman. Screenplay by John Michael
Hayes, based on the story by Charles
Bennett and D. B. Wyndham Lewis.
Starring: James Stewart, Doris Day,
Bernard Miles, Brenda De Banzie, Reggie
Nalder, Daniel Gélin.

1956 *The Wrong Man*
(a Warner Brothers-First National
Picture production)
Directed by Alfred Hitchcock. Produced
by Alfred Hitchcock and Herbert
Coleman. Screenplay by Maxwell
Anderson and Angus McPhail, based on
the story by Maxwell Anderson. Starring:
Henry Fonda, Vera Miles, Anthony
Quayle, Doreen Lang, Esther Minciotti,
Harold J. Stone.

1958 *Vertigo*
(a Paramount Picture)
Directed by Alfred Hitchcock. Produced
by Alfred Hitchcock and Herbert
Coleman. Screenplay by Alec Coppel and
Samuel Taylor, based on the novel *D'Entre
Les Morts* by Pierre Boileau and Thomas
Narcejac. Starring: James Stewart,
Kim Novak, Barbara Bel Geddes, Tom
Helmore, Henry Jones, Ellen Corby.

1959 *North by Northwest*
(an MGM Picture)
Directed by Alfred Hitchcock. Produced
by Alfred Hitchcock and Herbert
Coleman. Screenplay by Ernest Lehman.
Starring: Cary Grant, Eva Marie Saint,
James Mason, Jessie Royce Landis, Leo G.
Carroll, Martin Landau.

1960 *Psycho*
(a Paramount Picture)
Directed and produced by Alfred
Hitchcock. Screenplay by Joseph Stefano,
based on the novel by Robert Bloch.
Starring: Anthony Perkins, Janet Leigh,
Vera Miles, John Gavin, Martin Balsam,
Patricia Hitchcock, John McIntire,
Lurene Tuttle, Simon Oakland, Frank
Albertson, Vaughn Taylor.

1963 *The Birds*
(a Universal Release)
Directed and produced by Alfred
Hitchcock. Screenplay by Evan Hunter,
based on the short story by Daphne du
Maurier. Starring: Tippi Hedren, Rod
Taylor, Jessica Tandy, Suzanne Pleshette,
Veronica Cartwright, Doreen Lang.

1964 *Marnie*
(a Universal Release)
Directed and produced by Alfred
Hitchcock. Screenplay by Jay Presson
Allen, based on the novel by Winston
Graham. Starring: Tippi Hedren, Sean
Connery, Diane Baker, Louise Latham,
Martin Gabel, Bob Sweeney, Mariette
Hartley, Bruce Dern.

1966 *Torn Curtain*
(a Universal Release)
Directed and produced by Alfred
Hitchcock. Screenplay by Brian Moore.
Starring: Paul Newman, Julie Andrews,
Lila Kedrova, David Opatoshu, Ludwig
Donath, Tamara Toumanova.

1969 *Topaz*
(a Universal Release)
Directed by Alfred Hitchcock. Produced
by Alfred Hitchcock and Herbert
Coleman. Screenplay by Samuel Taylor,
based on the novel by Leon Uris. Starring:
Frederick Stafford, John Forsythe, Dany
Robin, John Vernon, Claude Jade, Philippe
Noiret, Michel Piccoli, Karin Dor.

1972 *Frenzy*
(a Universal Release)
Directed and produced by Alfred
Hitchcock. Screenplay by Anthony
Shaffer, based on the novel *Goodbye
Piccadilly, Farewell Leicester Square*
by Arthur Labern. Starring: Jon Finch,
Barry Foster, Barbara Leigh-Hunt,
Anna Massey, Alec McCowen, Vivien
Merchant, Billie Whitelaw, Clive Swift,
Bernard Cribbins.

1976 *Family Plot*
(a Universal Picture)
Directed and produced by Alfred
Hitchcock. Screenplay by Ernest Lehman,
based on the novel *The Rainbird Pattern*
by Victor Canning. Starring: Bruce Dern,
Barbara Harris, William Devane, Karen
Black, Ed Lauter, Nicholas Colasanto.

Books

Anobile, Richard A ., ed. *Alfred Hitchcock's PSYCHO*. New York: Universe Books, 1974.

Bankhead, Tallulah. *My Autobiography*. New York: Harper & Brothers, 1952.

Barbier, Philippe, and Jacques Moreau. *Album Photos: Alfred Hitchcock*. Paris: Pac, 1985.

Bazin, André. *Le Cinéma de la Cruauté*. Paris: Flammarion, 1987.

Behlmer, Rudy. *Memo from David 0. Selznick*. New York: Viking, 1972.

Bellour, Raymond. *L'Analyse du Film*. Paris: Editions Albatros, 1979.

Bjorkman, Stig, Jonas Sima, and Mams Trosten. *Bergman on Bergman*. Translated by Paul Britten. New York: Simon & Schuster. 1970/1973.

Brill, Leslie. *The Hitchcock Romance, Love and Irony in Hitchcock's Films*. Princeton, NJ: Princeton University Press, 1988.

Brown, Bryan. *The Alfred Hitchcock Movie Quiz Book*. New York: Perigee Books. 1986.

Brown, Peter Harry. *Kim Novak, Reluctant Goddess*. New York: St. Martin's Press, 1986.

Callan, Michael Feeny. *Sean Connery, His Life and Films*. London: W. H. Allen, 1983.

Carey, Cary. *Marlon Brando: The Only Contender*. New York: St. Martin's Press, 1985.

Condon, Paul and Jim Sangster. *The Complete Hitchcock*. London: Virgin Publishing Ltd., 1999.

Cotten, Joseph. *An Autobiography: Vanity Will Get You Nowhere*. New York: Mercury House, 1987.

Cronyn, Hume. *A Terrible Liar: Hume Cronyn, a Memoir*. New York: William Morrow, 1991.

DeMille, Cecil B. *The Autobiography of Cecil B. DeMille*. Edited by Donald Hayne. Englewood Cliffs, NJ: Prentice Hall, 1959.

Deutelbaum, Marshall, and Leland Poague, eds. *A Hitchcock Reader*. Ames, Iowa: Iowa State University Press, 1986.

Dietrich, Marlene. *Marlene Dietrich*. New York: Grove Press, 1987.

Douchet, Jean. *Hitchcock*. L'Herne, 1967. Paris: New Edition, 1985.

Ducout, Françoise. *Les Fantômes de Grand Central*. Paris: Pierre Hovay, 1988.

Durgnat, Raymond. *The Strange Case of Alfred Hitchcock, or The Plain Man's Hitchcock*. Cambridge, MA: MIT Press, 1974.

Estève, Michel, ed. *Alfred Hitchcock*. Paris: Minard, 1971.

Finler, Joel W. *Hitchcock in Hollywood*. New York: Continuum Publishing Group, 1992.

Freeman, David. *The Last Days of Alfred Hitchcock*. New York: Overlook Press, 1984.

Gielgud, John, in collaboration with John Miller and John Powell. *Gielgud, An Actor of His Time*. New York: Clarkson N. Porter, Inc., 1979.

Goldman, William. *Adventures in the Screen Trade*. New York: Warner Books, 1983.

Halley, Michael. *The Alfred Hitchcock Album*. Englewood Cliffs, NJ: Prentice Hall, 1981.

Halliwell, Leslie. *Halliwell's Filmgoer's and Video Viewer's Companion, 9th ed.* New York: Harper & Row, 1990.

——— *The Filmgoer's Book of Quotes*. London: Hart-Davis, MacGibbon, 1973.

Harris, Robert A., and Michael S. Lasky. *The Films of Alfred Hitchcock*. New York: Citadel Press, 1976.

Harris, Warren G. *Cary Grant: A Touch of Elegance*. Garden City, NY: Doubleday, 1987.

Haver, Donald. *David O. Selznick's Hollywood*. New York: Bonanza Books, 1980.

Head, Edith, and Paddy Calistro. *Edith Head's Hollywood*. New York: E.P. Dutton, 1983.

Hotchner, A. E. *Doris Day, Her Own Story*. New York: William Morrow, 1976.

Humphries, Patrick. *The Films of Alfred Hitchcock*. Greenwich, CT: Brom Books, 1986.

Kapsis, Robert E. *Hitchcock: The Making of a Reputation*. Chicago: University of Chicago Press, 1992.

Kazan, Elia. *Elia Kazan: A Life*. New York: Alfred A. Knopf, 1988.

Leff, Leonard J. *Hitchcock and Selznick*. New York: Weidenfeld & Nicolson, 1987.

Leitch, Thomas M. *Find the Director and Other Hitchcock Games*. Athens, GA: University of Georgia Press, 1991.

Maxford, Howard. *The A-Z of Hitchcock*. London: Batsford, 2002.

McGilligan, Patrick. *Backstory: Interviews With Screenwriters of Hollywood's Golden Age*. Berkeley: University of California Press, 1986.

McShane, Frank. *The Life of Raymond Chandler*. New York: E. P. Dutton, 1976.

Modelski, Tania. *The Women Who Knew Too Much: Hitchcock and Feminist Theory*. New York: Methuen, 1988.

Montcoffe, Francis. *Fenêtre sur Cour*. Paris: Nathan, 1990.

Morella, Joe, and Edward Z. Epstein. *Paul and Joanne: A Biography of Paul Newman and Joanne Woodward*. New York: Delacorte, 1988.

Morley, Sheridan. *James Mason, Odd Man Out*. New York: Harper & Row, 1989.

Olivier, Laurence. *Laurence Olivier: On Acting*. New York: Simon & Schuster, 1986.

Perry, George. *The Films of Alfred Hitchcock*. New York: Dutton/Vista, 1965.

——— *Hitchcock*. Garden City, NY: Doubleday, 1975.

Phillips, Gene D. *Alfred Hitchcock*. Boston: Twayne Publishing, 1984.

Powell, Michael. *Michael Powell: A Life in Movies and Art*. London: Heinemann, 1986.

Price, Theodore. *Hitchcock and Homosexuality*. Metuchen, NJ: Scarecrow Press, 1992.

Raubicheck, Walter, and Walter Srebnick, eds. *Hitchcock's Rereleased Films: From Rope to Vertigo*. Wayne, NE: Wayne State University Press, 1991.

Rebello, Stephen. *Alfred Hitchcock and the Making of Psycho*. New York: Dembner Books, 1990.

Rohmer, Eric, and Claude Chabrol. *Hitchcock: The First 44 Films*. New York: Frederick Ungar, 1979.

Rothman, William. *Hitchcock: The Murderous Gaze*. Cambridge, MA: Harvard University Press, 1982.

Ryall, Tom. *Alfred Hitchcock and the British Cinema*. Urbana, IL: University of Illinois Press, 1986.

Schoell, William. *Stay Out of the Shower*. New York: Dembner Books, 1985.

Sharff, Stephan. *Alfred Hitchcock's High Vernacular*. New York: Columbia University Press, 1991.

Simone, Sam P. *Hitchcock as Activist: Politics and the War Films*. Ann Arbor, MI: UMI Research Press, 1985.

Simsolo, Noel. *Alfred Hitchcock*. Paris: Seghers, 1979.

Sinyard, Neil. *The Films of Alfred Hitchcock*. New York: Galley Books, 1986.

Smith, Steven C. *A Heart at Fire's Center: The Life and Music of Bernard Herrmann*. Berkeley: University of California Press, 1991.

Spada, James. *Grace: The Secret Life of a Princess*. New York: Dolphin Books, 1987.

Spotto, Donald. *The Dark Side of Genius: The Life of Alfred Hitchcock*. Boston: Little, Brown, 1983.

——— *The Art of Alfred Hitchcock: 50 Years of His Motion Pictures*. New York: Anchor Books, 1976; new ed., 1992.

Tabori, George. *Monty*. New York: Arbor House, 1977.

Taylor, John Russell. *Hitch: The Life and Times of Alfred Hitchcock*. New York: Pantheon Books, 1978.

Truffaut, François. *Hitchcock/Truffaut*. New York: Simon & Schuster, 1983.

Villien, Bruno. *Hitchcock*. Paris: Rivages, 1985.

Weiss, Elisabeth. *The Silent Scream: Alfred Hitchcock's Soundtrack*. Cranbury, NJ: Associated University Presses, Inc., 1982.

Wood, Robin. *Hitchcock's Films Revisited*. New York: Columbia University Press, 1989.

Yacowar, Maurice. *Hitchcock's British Films*. Hamden, CT: Archon Books, 1977.

Zimmer, Jacques. *Alfred Hitchcock*. Paris: J'ai Lu, 1988.

Zizek, Slavoj, ed. *Tout ce que Vous Avez Toujours Voulu Savoir sur Lacan sans Jamais Oser le Demander à Hitchcock*. Paris: Navarin, 1980.

Periodicals

Anonymous. "Hitchcock." *Life*, 20 November 1939.

Anonymous. "Alfred Hitchcock: Director and Extra." *New York Times*, 28 October 1945.

Anonymous. "The Star in Hitch's Heaven." *News Review*, 10 March 1949.

Anonymous. "Hitchcock on a Train." *New York Daily News*, 27 November 1950.

Anonymous. "Hitchcock Chuckles Out of Disappearance." *Los Angeles Times*, 29 December 1955.

Anonymous. "Hitchcock Speaking." *Cosmopolitan*, October 1956.

Anonymous. "Hitchcock Gives View on Sex." *Los Angeles Times*, 21 December 1959.

Anonymous. "Hitchcock on the Tricks of his Trade." *People*, 20 May 1974.

Anonymous. "Hitchcock Shrugs Off Crippling Illnesses at 80 to Keep Working on Another Thriller." *The Star*, 5 February 1980.

Belcher, Jerry. "Master of Suspense Dead at 80." *Los Angeles Times*, 29 April 1980.

Blume, Mary. "Hitchcock Keeps His Cool on *Frenzy* Film Set." *Los Angeles Times*, 2 January 1972.

Cinefantastique Special Issue. "The Birds." Fall 1980.

Cinefantastique Special Issue. "Psycho." 10 October 1986.

Davis, Ivor. "Alfred Hitchcock Abhors Violence; Prefers Violence." *Los Angeles Times*, 7 September 1969.

Demonsablon, Philippe. "Lexique Mythologique pour l'œuvre de Hitchcock." *Cahiers du Cinéma*, August-September 1962.

Diehl, Digby. "Q&A, Alfred Hitchcock." *Los Angeles: Herald Examiner*, 25 June 1972.

Flatley, Guy. "I Tried to Be Discreet With That Nude Corpse." *New York Times*, 18 June 1972.

Goodman, Ezra. "The World Is Now With Hitchcock." *New York Herald Tribune*, 5 April 1942.

——— Untitled. *New York Daily News*, 29 March 1950.

Heffenan, Harold. "Hitch Views the Stars." *Milwaukee Journal*, 3 March 1963.

Heydt, Bruce. "The Master." *British Heritage*, June–July 1991.

Hildebrand, Harold. "Hitchcock Himself in Suspense 15 Years." *Los Angeles Herald Examiner*, 26 July 1959.

Hitchcock, Alfred. "The Woman Who Knows Too Much." *McCall's*, March 1956.

Hitchcock, Alfred and Dr. Fredric Wertham. "Redbook Dialogue." *Redbook*, April 1963.

Hitchcock, Alma, as told to Elizabeth Sherrill. *Everyone's Family Circle*, June 1958.

Hitchcock, Alma, as told to Martin Abramson. "My Husband Alfred Hitchcock Hates Suspense." *Coronet*, August 1964.

Hitchcock, Patricia, as told to Marya Saunders. "My Dad, the Jokester." *Citizen News*, 7 July 1963.

Hodenfield, Chris. "Muuuurder by the Babbling Brook." *Rolling Stone*, 29 July 1976.

Hopper, Hedda. "Alfred's Solution to Actor Problem." *Los Angeles Times*, 29 April 1962.

Kendall, Bob. "Hitchcock Speaks Out." *Hollywood Studios*, June 1976.

Knight, Arthur. "Killing Some Time With Alfred Hitchcock." *Los Angeles Times*, 23 July 1972.

——— "Conversation With Alfred Hitchcock." *Oui*, 2 February 1973.

Lehman, Ernest. "Hitch." *American Film*, 29 April 1980.

McBride, Joseph. "Nothing Will Ever Stop Hitch." *Variety*, 28 October 1975.

McClay, Howard. "'Fans Like Anxiety,' Hitchcock." *New York Daily News*, 20 July 1954.

Martin, Pete. "I Call on Alfred Hitchcock." *Saturday Evening Post*, 27 July 1957.

Maslin, Janet. "Alfred Hitchcock." *Boston After Dark*, 13 June 1972.

Miller, Mark Crispin. "In Memoriam: Alfred Hitchcock." *New Republic*, 26 July 1980.

Rau, Neil. "Hitchcock Explains His 'Little Suspense Game.'" *Los Angeles Herald Examiner*, 24 June 1956.

Reed, Rex. "Master of the Macabre." *South Land Sunday*, 30 July 1972.

Ruark, Robert C. Untitled. *Citizen News*, 23 February 1950.

Scheca, Philip K. "Hitch Your Mystery to Star, But Let Your Audience In on It." *Los Angeles Times*, 15 February 1953.

Schumach, Murray. "Hitchcock Insists Plot Is Vital to Suspense." *New York Times*, 12 February 1961.

Smith, Cecil. "Tea and Empathy With Hitchcock." *Los Angeles Times*, 24 September 1962.

Wakarska, Carol. "Hitch at the Helm." *Village Voice*, 8 September 1975.

Warhol, Andy, and Pat Hackett. "Hitchcock." *Interview Magazine*, July 1974.

Whitcomb, Jon, "Master of Mayhem." *Cosmopolitan*, October 1959.

Wixen, Joan. "Alfred Hitchcock: The Man Behind the Profile." *Family Circle*, May–June 1976.

Interviews

Laurent Bouzereau quoted a few excerpts from the following interviews, which were conducted for his documentaries about Hitchcock's movies:

Shadow of a Doubt*: Teresa Wright in Chapter II; *Saboteur**: Norman Lloyd in Chapter I and Robert Doyle in Chapter IV; *Rope**: Hume Cronyn in Chapter IV; *Strangers on a Train*†: Farley Granger in Chapter I; *Psycho**: Janet Leigh in Chapters II and III; *The Birds**: Rod Taylor in Chapter I and Tippi Hedren in Chapter II; *Marnie**: Jay Presson Allen in Chapter I and Louise Latham in Chapter II; *Topaz**: John Forsythe in Chapter III; *Frenzy**: Jon Finch in Chapter I, Anthony Shaffer in Chapters I and III, and Barry Foster in Chapter III; *Family Plot**: Bruce Dern in Chapter I, John Williams in Chapter IV, and Hilton Green in the conclusion.

* Universal Studios Home Entertainment
† Warner Home Video

about the author

Laurent Bouzereau is an award-winning filmmaker and best-selling author. He has written, directed, and produced many documentaries on the making of films by some of the world's most acclaimed filmmakers, including Steven Spielberg, Alfred Hitchcock, Brian De Palma, Martin Scorsese, George Lucas, Roman Polanski, and William Friedkin. His most recent work includes the acclaimed TCM / DreamWorks TV series *A Night at the Movies* and the book *The Art of Bond* (Abrams). Born in France, he now lives in Los Angeles.

Documentaries

The following films by Alfred Hitchcock adapted for home video contain documentaries written, directed, and produced by Laurent Bouzereau: *Saboteur, Shadow of a Doubt, Rope, The Trouble With Harry, Rear Window, The Man Who Knew Too Much, Psycho, The Birds, Marnie, Torn Curtain, Topaz, Frenzy, Family Plot,* and *Alfred Hitchcock Presents* (Universal Studios Home Entertainment); *Foreign Correspondent, Suspicion, Mr. and Mrs. Smith, Stage Fright, Strangers on a Train, Dial M for Murder, I Confess,* and *The Wrong Man* (Warner Home Video); and *To Catch a Thief* (Paramount Home Video).

Author's acknowledgments

To Alfred Hitchcock, family was everything. And I feel the same. I owe this book to:

My parents, Micheline and Daniel, my sisters, Cécile and Géraldine, my partner, Markus Keith . . . and our dog, Molly.

Jean-François Kowalski for his vision and for his trust in mine.

Kay McCauley for putting it all together.

Therese Eiben for making me sound like an American.

Adele Sparks for making it all official.

To my friends and colleagues at the different film studios, particularly Universal Studios Home Entertainment, Warner Home Video, and Paramount Home Video: thank you for allowing me to document the films of Alfred Hitchcock.

I've thanked them already but it won't hurt to mention them again: this book is the fruit of my friendship with Pat Hitchcock O'Connell and her amazing daughters, Mary, Katie, and Tere.

— Laurent Bouzereau

Book producer's acknowledgments

KNY Studio would like to thank Laurent Bouzereau, Patricia Hitchcock O'Connell, Katie Fiala, Tere Carruba, Mary Stone, Kay McCauley, Therese Eiben, Adele Sparks, Aiah Rachel Wieder, Isabelle Dartois, Vanessa López, Susanne Caesar, Universal, Paramount, Warner Brothers, Twentieth Century Fox, Laura Truffaut, Sam Levin, Linda Mehr, Barbara Hall and the staff of the Margareth Herrick Library, Photofest, Orren Zipper and his team at Park Lane Litho, Digital Fusion, Sarah McElwain, Coco Soodek, and J.P. Benitez. Very special thanks to Marie-Thérèse Kowalski and Chris Frieda.

— Jean-François Kowalski

TOP LEFT Hitchcock with his mother, Emma, and his daughter, Patricia, England, 1928

TOP RIGHT Hitchcock and Patricia going to Margate Beach, England, 1931

BOTTOM LEFT Hitchcock in Margate, circa 1930

BOTTOM RIGHT Emma; Patricia; Hitchcock; Alma's mother, Lucy; and Alma, 1929

credits

Photographs

Removable memorabilia

RIGHT Hitchcock playing with one of his Sealyham terriers at his Santa Cruz ranch, 1956